Directions in

Self-Access
Language
Learning

Directions in

Self-Access
Language
Learning

Edited by

David Gardner
and
Lindsay Miller

Hong Kong University Press
香港大學出版社

Hong Kong University Press
139 Pokfulam Road, Hong Kong

© Hong Kong University Press 1994

ISBN 962 209 362 0

Printed in Hong Kong by ColorPrint Production Company

Contents

Preface

As a concept, self-access language learning has been around for some time now. The notion, while not yet in its dotage, is certainly well beyond the first blush of youth. Despite this, there has been surprisingly little forward movement, either conceptually or pedagogically, since the concept began to attract serious attention in the early 1980s.

There is some evidence that this state of affairs is beginning to change. One such piece of evidence is this edited collection. The various contributions to the collection come from colleagues in a number of different institutions in Hong Kong. It is understandable then, that they should reflect a variety of viewpoints, approaches and philosophies. Despite (or, perhaps because of) this, I believe that the volume as a whole shows that self-access learning, despite it's age (and one would not want to push the metaphor too far) is experiencing something of a growth spurt. In addition to this volume, a healthy research programme is in train, and some of the more interesting studies are being carried out in Hong Kong.

While the principal aim of this volume is to act as a practical guide to preparing students for independent learning, I believe that the papers advance the cause of self-access learning conceptually as well as pedagogically. The conceptual strength of the papers takes the volume beyond the realm of the 'wish list' for the practitioner who is currently engaged in, or wishing to be involved in, self-access learning.

For many years, I have argued the case for concepts such as learner centredness, learner autonomy, and learner independence, all of which differ in a number of critical ways. However, they also share a common philosophy, and a common focus on the learner. To that extent they belong to the same pedagogical family. It is therefore a source of considerable pride to me that this volume, and the conference from which it sprang, have had considerable input and support from the University of Hong Kong in general, and the English Centre in particular. I look forward, in the years to come, to lending my own energies, such as they are, to furthering the cause of self-access learning within the community of language learners in Hong Kong and beyond.

Professor David Nunan
Director
English Centre
The University of Hong Kong

Introduction

The past five years has seen an explosion of interest in self-access language learning in many parts of the world. This interest is most obvious in such places as the Centre de Recherches et d'Applications Pédagogiques en Langues in France, the Self-Study Centre of the Bell College, Saffron Walden and the Language Centre at Cambridge University. Within Southeast Asia, Hong Kong has become a centre of expertise in self-access as a result of the large-scale development of independent learning largely promoted by government funding of language enhancement.

The rapid development of self-access in Hong Kong has been assisted by the Hong Kong Association of Self-Access Learning and Development (HASALD) which was established in 1992 to act as a talking shop for those interested in self-access learning. It has maintained an active membership of academics, company trainers and school teachers who feel a need to swap ideas on practical issues related to the provision of self-access facilities. Most of the papers in this book are written by members of HASALD and demonstrate the wide ranging interests of the group members. Many of the authors have experience within an international context as language teachers, material writers and administrators, others have detailed knowledge of the local educational system and the particular learning styles of Chinese students.

Self-access language learning is often seen as a method in itself, however, as the papers in this book demonstrate, a variety of methods can be adopted in dealing with similar learners in similar situations. The papers presented here are about practical issues and are divided into four sections: Approaches to Self-Access, Learner Training, Materials, and Evaluating Self-Access.

The first section, Approaches to Self-Access, consists of four papers dealing with some of the different approaches that can be taken to self-access. Phil Benson outlines the basis of a critical theory of self-access language learning as a consumer commodity in his paper 'Self-Access Systems as Information Systems: Questions of Ideology and Control'. He describes what might be involved in developing a theoretical framework within which a self-access centre can be used in directing learner autonomy. Benson proposes that self-access systems can be seen as information systems within the framework of 'social semiotics'.

In the second paper Richard Farmer offers a case study to exemplify and justify the reasons behind his approach to implementing self-access in a tertiary institute. 'The Limits of Learner Independence' outlines the problems of introducing independent language learning to Hong Kong students and Farmer describes how he has adopted a 'shallow-end' approach. He describes how learner feedback on an independent learning programme was instrumental in implementing changes to accommodate the learners' expectations. The author extends a cautious note as to how far we can expect learners to drop their old style of teacher-centred learning in favour of complete self-directed learning. However, he also offers suggestions on how learners can be encouraged to modify their learning behaviours in favour of more independence.

Terence Pang offers yet another approach in implementing self-access as a mode of learning. In 'A Self-Directed Project: A Critical Humanistic Approach to Self-Access' Pang describes how his students are encouraged to view the self-access centre as one of many facilities which enable them to reach their goal of presenting a project. The learners are put into groups and given a certain time to investigate a problem or situation. They may use any method to obtain information and assistance with the language of their presentation (English). Pang mentions how action research is the most appropriate method of assessment of such a programme and how the feasibility of the programme rests with the consensus of all the participants.

In the last paper in this section Kathy Hayward introduces the concept of writing centres as part of self-access centres. Hayward's paper 'Self-Access Writing Centres' describes how writing centres have been established in two tertiary institutions in Hong Kong. In the first example the writing centre is an entity in itself, in the second example it is placed within a self-access centre. Hayward argues the benefits of developing a writing centre as a way of offering support for language learners and how this can be of particular use if included as part of a self-access centre.

The theme of the five papers in the second section of the book is Learner Training. All of the papers describe programmes which can be used to help learners understand more about their language learning needs. The first two papers describe how general language training can be implemented, the third paper describes learner logs as a tool to aid learner autonomy, while the last two papers in the section focus on specific skill areas: speaking and pronunciation.

The second section starts with Winnie Or's paper 'Helping Learners Plan and Prepare for Self-Access Learning'. Or gives specific examples of how a tutor can help a learner make informed choices about what to learn in a self-access environment. She points out that learners often perceive their language learning problems as vast and unmanageable. However, with the help of a trained tutor the learning objectives can be broken down into manageable and operational sub-goals to help learners select what to work on and how to direct their language learning efforts more economically. By helping the learner in this way Or points out that we not only help them with a strategy for their own language learning, but we enhance their motivation to learn by making the process more manageable.

'What Is the Fare to the Land of Effective Language Learning?' by Beatrice Ma looks at general learner training in a slightly different way, this time from the point of view of a dedicated programme of events to help the learner become orientated towards self-access language learning. Ma describes a seven day programme which encourages learners to reconsider how they learn a language. The learners consider such things as their attitudes to and beliefs about learning a language and what sorts of knowledge can help them. At the end of the programme the learners are asked to undertake a series of language learning activities which they monitor in a log book. Ma explains that the complex and flexible nature of study at tertiary level requires learners to become more independent and one way of helping them achieve this independence is through the FARE programme.

Elaine Martyn's paper, 'Self-Access Logs: Promoting Self-Directed Learning' documents an on-going project which looks at providing learners with guidance while also offering autonomy. The development of a suitable log which supports students without being prescriptive has gone through a number of stages each of which has been carefully documented through student and teacher feedback. The logs themselves have been analysed after learners have finished with them and the results have been used to continue the process of evolving the log towards a flexible self-access learning tool. This paper discusses learner attitudes towards using a log and also comments on teachers' attitudes to the utility and efficacy of the approach.

The next two papers in this section show how specific skills can be catered for in learner training. Deirdre Moynihan Tong presents a case study under the title of 'Training Learners for Independence'. This paper describes how learners can be encouraged to investigate their language learning strategies and in particular how these strategies can be used to improve speaking skills. Moynihan Tong outlines ten elements of a programme she has worked on and comments on the useful feedback the learners provided when undertaking this programme. The programme relies on getting learners to understand what strategies they already have at their disposal to improve their speaking. It then helps learners find out about materials they can use to improve their speaking skills and how to evaluate their performance. She concludes that although the study reported on was only a pilot study the reactions of the learners and their comments indicate that they appreciated this type of learner training and that it appears to develop the learners' confidence in learning independently.

The last paper in this section is by Pamela Rogerson-Revell and Lindsay Miller. This paper is on 'Developing Pronunciation Skills through Self-Access Learning'. Rogerson-Revell and Miller describe a strategy for learner-training with pronunciation. This includes sensitizing learners to their pronunciation problems by means of a questionnaire and tests. Examples of the type of questionnaire and tests that could be used in this diagnostic period are included in the paper. The authors then take the reader through the decision stages that are involved in building a strategy for improving the student's pronunciation. The decision making involved is clearly exemplified and could easily be used in any self-access centre. The authors describe what they feel are the essential elements of good pronunciation materials, these include activities that emphasize awareness, explanation, recognition, production and self-correction. The paper ends with a review of some of the most popular pronunciation books on the market and recommendations for setting up a pronunciation section within a self-access centre.

The third section of this book, Materials, contains five papers which look at specific issues concerning the provision of materials for self-access learning. David Gardner's paper on 'Creating Simple Interactive Video for Self-Access' considers the difficulties of using video for self-access learning, particularly the problems of passive viewing. He discusses possible solutions and suggests that simple interactive video which re-purposes already published video tape and is developed by language teachers not technicians is a viable short and medium term solution. He also discusses the advantages of a simple tape-based system over more sophisticated interactive videodisc packages.

In her paper 'Materials Production for Self-Access Centres in Secondary Schools' Janice Tibbetts considers the practicalities of producing suitable materials within the constraints of a minimal budget and severe restrictions on teachers' time. She suggests that the most successful way of beginning the process is to remain aware of the ultimate aim of the self-access centre but also to work within a very narrow focus of materials. This gives both learners and teachers an opportunity to become accustomed to a new approach to learning. Tibbetts describes a successful materials production project within her own school, commenting on the target group, the focus of the materials and the generation of materials as well as practical issues of storage, indexing and utilization.

Julie Forrester in her paper 'Self-Access Language Learning for Secondary School Students' describes the development of the self-access component of an intensive language course which was designed by the British Council to help learners cope with the gap between Chinese medium secondary schools and English medium tertiary institutions. Forrester describes how self-access was integrated with the classroom based elements of the course and also comments on the practical issues involved in the production, organisation and supervision of large quantities of self-access materials at relatively short notice.

Lynne Flowerdew's paper entitled 'Incorporating Aspects of Style and Tone in Self-Access CALL Courseware' describes how she used an error analysis approach in the design of a computer assisted self-access package aimed at improving students' letter and résumé writing specifically for job seeking purposes. Flowerdew's analysis showed that in students' letters errors of style and tone outnumbered those of lexis and grammar and were potentially offensive to the reader. This paper discusses how features of style and tone have been incorporated into the various exercises within the package. It also looks at the conflict between the linguistic expectations of prospective employers and the language teacher's concern for clear and concise writing. This is a cross-cultural issue which emerged during the planning and design of the materials.

Linda Mak, in her paper 'From English Teacher to Producer', discusses, from her perspective as an ELT teacher, her experiences in the development of a multimedia computer simulation in collaboration with computer and media specialists. Mak describes in detail the preparation, production and revision processes of the software development and highlights the triumphs and pitfalls she encountered, which serve as a useful warning to all would-be developers. She gives us a broader perspective on the development of multimedia language learning software by listing the issues that need to be resolved before beginning such a project. Despite warning that teachers should think twice before embarking on a similar project, Mak's willingness to do it all over again shines through.

The last section of this book, Evaluating Self-Access, contains two papers which evaluate self-access in very different ways. Marian Star discusses how to obtain feedback on a self-access centre. In 'Learning to Improve: Evaluating Self-Access Centres', Star outlines how with large amounts of funding being given to establish self-access centres we have to monitor them to see if they meet the needs for which they were established. The author describes a case study where learners were asked to evaluate the facilities of a self-access centre by means of questionnaires. The results of these questionnaires are presented and the author explains how changes have been implemented because of the feedback received. Star reminds us that self-access centres should be seen as evolving environments and that evaluation of such facilities should be an on-going process.

Lindsay Miller and David Gardner in their paper, 'Directions for Research into Self-Access Language Learning', evaluate not what has been happening in the field of self-access but rather what needs to happen if future developments are to be based on a firm footing. They list a number of reasons why there is an urgent need for quality research to be conducted into various aspects of self-access learning. They suggest areas within the field of self-access learning where further research is needed and list suggestions for directions the research might take. The lists are not intended to be comprehensive but rather to stimulate discussion and to encourage practitioners and would-be practitioners of self-access to adopt an active research role.

Contributors

David Gardner is a Senior Language Instructor in the English Centre of the University of Hong Kong. He has taught EFL and ESP at secondary and tertiary levels in France, Saudi Arabia, England and now in Hong Kong. His main interests are the use of interactive video, video and computer-assisted learning in the learning of languages especially in self-access mode.

Lindsay Miller is a University Lecturer in the English Department of City Polytechnic of Hong Kong. His main areas of research interest are in self-access language learning, English for science and technology and materials writing. He is co-editor with David Nunan of *New Ways in Teaching Listening*.

Phil Benson teaches in the English Centre at the University of Hong Kong. He has also taught in Algeria, Kuwait, Seychelles, Malaysia and Japan. His research interests are in self-access, language and ideology and world Englishes.

Richard Farmer is a Principal Lecturer in the Department of English, Hong Kong Polytechnic, where he is co-ordinator of the English Language Study-Centre. He has previously taught in England, Kuwait, Jordan and Somalia and has written textbooks for use in China. His main areas of interest include self-access language learning, learner independence and teacher training.

Lynne Flowerdew teaches EAP and business and technical communication skills courses in the Language Centre of the Hong Kong University of Science and Technology. Her areas of interest include CALL for self-access use, concordanced-based materials writing and corpus linguistics. She is co-editor of *Entering Text*, the conference proceedings of a seminar on corpus linguistics and lexicography at the Hong Kong University of Science and Technology.

Julie Forrester has been teaching EFL for the British Council for eight years, first in Oman and now in Hong Kong. Her current interests are teacher training, reading strategies and materials writing for self-access in secondary schools.

Kathy Hayward is a Lecturer in the English Language Teaching Unit of the Chinese University of Hong Kong where she has set up and directs a writing centre within the Independent Learning Centre. She has also set up a writing centre at Hong Kong Baptist College, and has taught EFL in China, Italy, England and Iran. Her research interests include coherence and cohesion in writing, and writing in self-access.

Beatrice Ma teaches at the English Language Unit of the Chinese University of Hong Kong. Her main research interests are in language learner training for adult learners and learning styles.

Linda Mak is a Language Instructor in the English Language Teaching Unit of the Chinese University of Hong Kong. Her main areas of research interest are computer-mediated communication, collaborative learning networks and computer-assisted language learning in the self-access mode.

Elaine Martyn is a Language Instructor at the English Centre of the University of Hong Kong. She has been teaching EFL for ten years at secondary and tertiary levels in Nigeria, Pakistan, the People's Republic of China and now in Hong Kong. Her current research interests are in the implementation of self-access learning and spoken discourse analysis.

Deirdre Moynihan Tong is an English Language Instructor in the English Language Study-Centre of Hong Kong Polytechnic. She has been teaching EFL and ESP in Hong Kong for six years. Her main areas of interest are learner independence, learner training, learner strategies, self-access materials development and English for business.

Winnie W.F. Or teaches EAP and Technical Communication courses in the Language Centre of the Hong Kong University of Science and Technology. She is involved in the development of the self-access centre. Her main interests are in the general area of learner training, such as learning styles and strategies and also autonomy and culture.

Terence T.T. Pang is currently Co-ordinator of the Self-Access Centre and a University Lecturer of English at Lingnan College, Hong Kong. He formerly taught at the Institute of Languages at the University of New South Wales, Australia and at the Language Institute of the City Polytechnic of Hong Kong. His interests are in learner autonomy, learning styles, genre analysis, oral proficiency scaling and the ideology of language pedagogy.

Pamela Rogerson-Revell is a University Lecturer in Business English at City Polytechnic of Hong Kong. She is co-author of two books published by Cambridge University Press: *Speaking Clearly* and *Business Speaking*.

Marian Star is an Acting Senior Lecturer in the English Department of the Institute of Language in Education. Her teaching and research interests are in the areas of curriculum and classroom practice, self-access language learning and learner strategies.

Janice Tibbetts is a teacher in a government secondary school in Hong Kong. She has been teaching English language, literature, media studies, EFL, ESL and ESP for seventeen years at secondary, pre-tertiary and tertiary levels in England, Papua New Guinea and now in Hong Kong. Her main interests are the development of learner autonomy by means of self-access centres and computer-assisted language learning. Her other interests are vocational education, materials writing and learner strategies.

—— **Acknowledgements** ══

We would like to thank the English Centre of the University of Hong Kong for its donation towards part of the cost of this publication. We would also like to thank Barbara Clarke and the staff of Hong Kong University Press for their help and support throughout.

David Gardner and Lindsay Miller
Hong Kong, 1994

Section One

Approaches to Self-Access

1

Self-Access Systems as Information Systems: Questions of Ideology and Control[1]

Phil Benson, English Centre, The University of Hong Kong

INTRODUCTION

Until recently, self-access language learning facilities were discussed mainly in terms of support for projects in self-directed and autonomous learning (Holec 1981; Riley 1982; Dickinson 1987). But in the last few years, self-access has become an issue in its own right, and attention has shifted to organizational aspects of setting up and running self-access centres (Little 1989; Sheerin 1989, 1991; Mitchener 1991; McCall 1992; Moore 1992; Carvalho 1993; Miller and Rogerson-Revell 1993). In much of this literature, underlying philosophies of learning take second place to the solution of practical problems, and learner autonomy increasingly appears as a purely optional or ideal goal. Consequently, those concerned with autonomy in language learning may see little scope in the day-to-day organization of self-access for the kind of critical practice which might lead to this goal.

In this paper, I want to argue that self-access organization is not really a practical problem at all, and that it bears a significant relationship to learning. In order to do this, I will attempt to outline the basis of a critical theory which can relate questions of organization to underlying philosophies of learning by dealing with the social and ideological implications of self-access systems of different kinds. The first part of the paper is a critique of 'practical self-access' as an approach which, I will argue, leaves language learners prey to an ideology of 'language learning as commodity consumption' and does little to promote learner autonomy. In the second part of the paper I will try to outline the elements of a theory of self-access and some of the issues which it would need to address. In the course of this discussion, I also want to explore the relevance of social semiotic analysis of self-access systems as *information* systems as a theoretical framework which can accommodate the social character of organizational systems.

DO WE NEED A THEORY OF SELF-ACCESS ORGANIZATION?

In order to answer this question, I need to discuss briefly the nature of practical and critical approaches to social activity and their relationship to ideology.

The term 'ideology' is increasingly used in the context of education to refer to beliefs about learning. Sturtridge (1992:4), for example, refers to the ideologies which underlie self-access systems as 'the basic beliefs about learning which are held by those who set up the system'. In this paper, however, I will use the term in a wider sense to indicate the ways in which beliefs about learning are embedded in social processes. In this sense, ideology refers to fundamental conceptions of society, and the way that it works, which condition thought about language and language learning. The relationship between ideology and language learning is complex since it can also be said that language *is* ideology (Kress and Hodge 1979), and that a great deal of learning consists in learning ideologies through the medium of language. A full discussion of these issues would not be relevant here, but one point that I would like to pursue is the social function of ideology.

Ideologies can be seen as sets of ideas which represent the interests of particular social groups as the interests of all. Ideologies of dominant groups, therefore, tend to represent the social relations which underpin their dominance as natural, inevitable or incontestable. In modern capitalist societies, the incontestability of dominant ideas is characteristically expressed in the notion of 'common sense'. 'Practicality' is also a highly ideological notion, since it is generally based on the idea that problems can be solved without reference to the legitimacy of underlying ideological assumptions. Critical approaches, on the other hand, tend to question this legitimacy by referring back to the social processes which produce common sense notions. The relevance of this to a discussion of self-access organization and learner autonomy will be clear. Practical approaches to problems of self-access organization are unlikely to lead automatically to learner autonomy, because autonomy implies a restructuring of social relations in learning. Learner autonomy can only be the product of a critical practice that questions the legitimacy of existing social relations and the categorisations which support them.

For the English language, dominant ideologies of learning are conditioned by the existence of a large-scale industry engaged in the production and sale of language and language learning on a world scale. In the terms outlined earlier, beliefs about language learning are embedded within social processes of commodity production, and conditioned by the fundamental conception that commodity production serves the general interest by satisfying social needs through individual consumption. Again, a full treatment of these issues would not be relevant here (for a detailed discussion see Phillipson [1992]), and I will only summarize five key aspects of the process:

1. The marketing of EFL and ESL involves the production and sale of technology and learning materials (textbooks, video, audio and computer software).
2. Language learning itself (in the form of language courses, language teaching and expertise) is packaged and sold as a commodity on the world market.
3. Languages themselves are objectified and represented metaphorically as commodities with different relative values — as 'exports' which are converted into added 'value' for countries (as access to markets and power) and individuals (as social mobility) who are able to 'acquire' them.
4. Language learning is also objectified and cut up into discrete skills (pronunciation, listening, etc.) to be marketed as commodities in their own right.
5. The construction of language and language learning as commodities is accompanied by a division of language users into producers (monolingual 'native speakers') and consumers (bilingual 'non-native speakers'). This involves the ideological construction of the 'language learner' as a consumer of commodities.

The transformation of language learning into commodity production is a complex process involving both the actual production and sale of commodities and the metaphorical representation of processes as things. But metaphorical representation operates with real social force. In terms of dominant ideologies of language learning, to become a speaker of a language other than one's mother tongue is to become a 'learner' of that language and hence a potential consumer of commodities. To do otherwise would be to acquire language without at the same time acquiring any of its 'value'. It is in this sense that I referred earlier to the ways in which beliefs are embedded in social processes. To a very large extent, beliefs about language learning embody fundamental notions of capitalist commodity production. This is not to say that thinking about language learning slavishly follows dominant social and economic ideas. It is rather that dominant ideas form a coercive set of categorisations which condition that thinking. It is inconceivable, therefore, that a concept such as learner autonomy, which fundamentally contradicts the notion of the language learner as a passive consumer of knowledge, could be introduced into current language learning practice without a critique of these categorisations.

To return to self-access, five general operating principles of 'practical self-access', corresponding to the five aspects of language learning as commodity consumption listed above, can be identified:

1. Self-access centres often depend on the commodities of language learning, replacing teachers and classrooms with technology and learning materials. Other resources, especially human resources, tend to play a secondary role.

2. Corresponding to the packaging of language learning as a commodity is the notion of the self-access centre as the major resource for independent learning. An emphasis on learning programmes, pathways and objectives as well as concern with explicit advice and instructions, reflect a tendency for self-access centres to try to substitute themselves for language courses. The idea of independent language learning as a journey into the unknown seems to be anathema.

3. The metaphorical representation of language as a commodity appears in self-access as a concern with the learner's needs, which tend to be evaluated in functional terms (Business English, English at work, ESP, etc.). When learners express more general social needs (e.g. 'to communicate with foreigners') they are often encouraged to be 'more specific'.

4. The segmentation of language competence into skills is often highly apparent in self-access centres. Materials are classified and displayed according to marketing categories. These categories are also used in 'needs' analysis. By interacting with learning materials in this way, users of a self-access centre are strongly encouraged to construct their own identities as learners in terms specified by the language learning industry. Moreover, an emphasis on identifiable skill development may present a limited view of language competence. Often language skills are separated from their implementation in social contexts, reinforcing the distinction between language 'learner' and language 'user'.

5. In many self-access centres the roles of producer and consumer of language are quite rigidly defined. As a rule, the learner's role in a self-access centre is simply to learn. Few self-access centres accord any controlling role to freely organized groups of learners. It seems that practically-organized self-access centres do not see their users in any other role than that of individual consumers of language learning products.

These features of 'practical self-access' do not, of course represent an explicit set of beliefs about self-access language learning. They are synthesized from observations of self-access in practice and represent spontaneous solutions to what are perceived as practical problems. Such solutions are often a response to financial constraints and institutional demands to implement 'autonomous learning' quickly, cheaply and with a minimum commitment to ongoing resourcing. A similar picture also emerges, however, in practical guides to self-access (cf. Sheerin [1989]). Practical solutions to organizational problems are difficult to criticize because their practicality appears to be self-justifying. What I have tried to suggest is that practical approaches necessarily detach self-access from the goal of learner autonomy. Sheerin (1989:3) for example, argues:

The primary aim of such [self-access study] facilities is to enable learning to take place independently of teaching. Students are able to choose and use self-access material on their own and the material gives them the ability to correct or assess their own performance. By using such a self-access facility, students are able to direct their own learning.

It does not necessarily follow, however, that simply by using a self-access centre on their own, students will be able to direct their own learning, especially if self-access facilities are organized in ways that promote an ideology of language learning as commodity consumption.

From what I have argued so far, it may seem as if self-access itself is an inappropriate medium for the promotion of self-directed learning and learner autonomy. But self-access centres are not always organized on practical grounds. What remains to be developed is a systematic approach that takes account of the ideological implications of organizational solutions in order to firmly link self-access to the goal of learner autonomy. In the second part of this paper I will attempt to outline what might be involved in the development of such an approach.

ELEMENTS OF A THEORY OF SELF-ACCESS

In general terms, the aim of a theory of self-access would be to define how the organization of learning resources and environments interacts with the process of learning. In narrower terms, it would deal with the relationship between self-access systems and autonomy in learning. In a sense, the earlier critique of practical self-access covered the negative aspects of such a theory. It should also be possible to approach the issue positively, however, by proposing specific organizational criteria for the promotion of autonomy in practice. I would not pretend to be able to define a theory of self-access in this paper — this could only emerge from extensive discussion and practice. What I will attempt is to suggest a possible theoretical framework for considering problems of self-access organization and to discuss some of its key terms.

It is worth noting from the outset that the concepts of self-access, self-directed learning and learner autonomy and their interrelationships in language learning remain ill-defined both in the literature and in the practice of self-access. A clearer definition of these concepts and the levels at which they operate is needed. As a working model, there might be general agreement that autonomy represents a goal, self-directed learning a means of achieving it, and self-access an environment within which it can be achieved. In the context of language learning, autonomy could be defined as a social transformation of the individual from 'language learner' to 'language user'. In this case, it may be useful to think of self-access organization in terms of interventions at the environmental level to promote this transformation in the individual's social identity.

An implication of this line of argument is the need for a social dimension within a theory of self-access. Riley (1986) has suggested one possible framework for this in an analysis of self-access in terms of roles. This does not, however, lead to a full theory of organization, which must incorporate analysis of both technical and human resources at a systemic level. One approach which may lead in this direction is offered by social semiotic analysis.

The term 'social semiotics' apparently originates with Halliday (1978:2) who describes social reality as 'an edifice of meanings' to be analysed in semiotic terms as an 'information system'. In a much fuller development of the concept, Hodge and Kress (1988) apply social semiotic analysis to 'texts' employing a variety of linguistic, visual, spatial, dress and architectural codes. Key elements in the methodology are an emphasis on the inter-dependence of different codes in semiotic systems and a concern with ideology and the social context of communication. It seems that social semiotics has not so far been applied to the analysis of organization, but the notion of self-access systems as information systems constituted by acts of communication is one which appears to work well in the light of my earlier description of self-access as an intervention into the social context of learning.

In semiotic terms, self-access systems construct and convey information about language learning through a variety of agencies including the architectural design and layout of self-access centres, the selection and physical arrangement of resources, catalogues, indexes, handouts, and face-to-face contact with self-access organizers or helpers. Each of these agencies employs one or more of a variety of codes (spatial, visual, organizational, print, speech) within specific situational contexts. Semiotic analysis thus provides tools and vocabulary to analyse how self-access systems work. In particular, these tools permit analysis of apparently diverse activities such as the planning of a self-access system, materials selection and design, cataloguing, counselling and learner training within a single methodological framework, as different means of achieving similar goals. More importantly, by dealing with the social dimension of organizational systems (what they say about the social system and how this information is received), social semiotic analysis may lead to a better understanding of the ways in which self-access systems communicate information about their users' roles in the learning process.

Some of the most important information communicated by self-access systems about the social system of learning concerns the power of the institutions (ultimately the language learning industry and the general system of commodity production) within which self-access operates. It is widely accepted that highly efficient, high-tech self-access operations are not necessarily the best, especially if they lack a human dimension. An analysis of such systems in terms of power would suggest that what is gained in terms of access to resources may be lost in terms of learners' access to their own learning, because language and language learning are presented as reified and alien objects within a highly complex and powerful system.

The reaction of users to highly organized systems is unpredictable, however. The way in which information systems are 'read' depends upon previous experiences and positions in relation to the underlying social system. For some users, highly organized systems may be intimidating. For others, especially those who have already internalized many of the categories and assumptions of the language learning industry, they may represent a usable resource. In either case, it is unlikely that autonomy will be the result. On the other hand, learners cannot be expected to abandon established learning practices altogether, especially where these are seen to be effective in the mastery of mechanical aspects of communication. One solution to this dilemma might lie in a consideration of the value of disruptions to established systems.

By disruptions I mean any intervention which modifies or alters social relationships within a system. Organizational systems rarely allow for their own disruption, since they are ideally based on principles of clarity, logical structure, efficiency and productivity. But self-access systems which aim to promote self-direction and autonomy may do well to question such principles. It has been suggested, for example, (Riley 1986; Benson 1992) that efficient library-type information retrieval systems are not necessarily what is needed for cataloguing self-access resources if the aim is to encourage users to explore and reflect on the role of learning resources in their own learning. In other areas of organization too, openness to criticism and creativity may be important, which means ensuring that the system as a whole is open to user input. Some attempts in this direction are currently being made in learner preparation courses at the University of Hong Kong (Benson 1993) where, instead of being trained how to use learning resources and make choices from pre-defined categories, students are encouraged to create their own categories, criticize resources and devise methods of using them which meet their own goals.

In developing a theory of self-access, there would also be a need to consider questions of control and solidarity. The issue of control arises because learner autonomy involves not only attitudinal and behavioural changes, but also a transformation of the social identity of the learner. When learners choose resources from a self-access centre and use them without the assistance of a teacher, they are not necessarily engaged in self-directed activity because these resources may themselves be other-directed to a very large extent. Learners are always and inevitably subject to other-direction up until the point where they are able to subject the agencies of other-direction to their own control. A theory of self-access would, therefore, need to look at how self-access systems can encourage their users to take control of significant aspects of the systems themselves. This may call for a reconsideration of the roles of teachers, learners, helpers, organizers and so on because these roles are themselves predicated upon relations of power and control. It goes without saying perhaps that this reconsideration might be problematic since any increase in learner control may result in a corresponding decrease in institutional control for which teachers and organizers may need to be prepared (Littlejohn 1985; Sturtridge 1992).

Solidarity in self-access is related to the issue of control and is used here to refer to the friendships or other informal structures which exist among learners and help them in their work. It is the social character of language which makes solidarity an important factor in language learning, but solidarity also enters into relationships between the institution and the individual engaged in self-access. By helping users of a self-access centre to develop study partnerships and groups, we may be able to furnish them with 'power bases' from which they can extend their control over their own learning and the system in general. The ways in which self-access systems can facilitate the development of learner solidarity would, therefore, be an important area of concern for a theory of self-access. Without learner solidarity it seems unlikely that very much could be achieved in the area of learner control.

CONCLUSION

Studying language in a self-access centre is not equivalent to self-directed language learning, nor does it lead directly to autonomy in learning. The ways in which self-access is organized have a significant influence on the kinds of learning that take place, and this influence is open to investigation at a theoretical level. I have suggested that social semiotic analysis of self-access systems as information systems could constitute a basis for such investigation, but other approaches might be equally productive. Perhaps the most important point is to recognize that there is more than one way to organize self-access (cf. Pang and Farmer in this volume), and that the only real test of a system is whether or not it is able to achieve the goals which it sets for itself.

NOTE

1. I would like to emphasize that this paper is intended to be as critical of my own work in self-access as it is of others'. I am especially grateful to William Littlewood and Alastair Pennycook for comments and discussions which have helped considerably to clarify my thoughts.

REFERENCES

Benson, P. 1992. 'Self-access for self-directed learning'. *Hong Kong Papers in Linguistics and Language Teaching* 15:31–7.

———. 1993. 'How to be a better language learner: a learner preparation programme for self-access'. Paper given at the ILEC Conference on Language and Learning, University of Hong Kong, December 1993.

Carvalho, D. 1993. *Self-Access: Appropriate Material.* Manchester: British Council.

Dickinson, L. 1987. *Self-Instruction in Language Learning.* Cambridge: Cambridge University Press.

Halliday, M.A.K. 1978. *Language as Social Semiotic: The Social Interpretation of Language and Meaning.* London: Edward Arnold.

Hodge, R. and Kress G.R. 1988. *Social Semiotics.* Cambridge: Polity Press.

Holec, H. 1981. *Autonomy and Foreign Language Learning.* London: Pergamon.

Kress, G.R. and Hodge, R. 1979. *Language as Ideology.* London: Routlege and Kegan Paul.

Little, D., ed. 1989. *Self-Access Systems for Language Learning.* Dublin: Authentik/CILT.

Littlejohn, A. 1985. 'Learner choice in language study'. *ELT Journal* 39(4):253–61.

McCall, J. 1992. *Self-Access: Setting Up a Centre.* Manchester: British Council.

Miller, L. and Rogerson-Revell, P. 1993. 'Self-access systems'. *ELT Journal* 47(3):228–33.

Mitchener, D. 1991. 'Setting up a self-access unit'. *MET* 17:(3) and (4):70–
    1.

Moore, C. 1992. *Self-Access: Appropriate Technology*. Manchester: Brit-
    ish Council.

Phillipson, R. 1992. *Linguistic Imperialism*. Oxford: Oxford University
    Press.

Riley, P. 1982. 'Learners' lib: experimental autonomous learning scheme',
    in M. Geddes and G. Sturtridge (eds.) *Individualisation*. London: Mod-
    ern English Publications.

———. 1986. 'Who's who in self-access'. *TESOL France News* 6(2):23–
    34.

Sheerin, S. 1989. *Self-Access*. Oxford: Oxford University Press.

———. 1991. 'Self-access'. *Language Teaching* 24(3):143–57.

Sturtridge, G. 1992. *Self-Access: Preparation and Training*. Manchester:
    British Council.

CHAPTER 2

The Limits of Learner Independence in Hong Kong

Richard Farmer, English Language Study-Centre, Hong Kong Polytechnic

INTRODUCTION

Since self-access embodies a learner-centred approach, it seems appropriate to start with some of the initial reactions which learners had to the introduction of learner independence in the programmes of study at the English Language Study-Centre, Hong Kong Polytechnic.

'I prefer a teachers to teach me in the whole programme because he/she can know what I need and the progress in learning.'

'I prefer the teacher encourage me talking to speak a lot.'

'I would like to have a teacher with me in the whole lesson but not always goes away and let us alone.'

'Small group learning with needs analysis are useful for studying English.'

This paper describes the body of learners attending programmes at the Study-Centre and discusses why they depend to such an extent on teacher direction. It explains how we have attempted to redress this through introducing, very gradually, certain features of learner independence and how far we have had to limit this objective in the light of student response. The extent to which learner independence has been successfully implemented is briefly considered and the paper concludes with an outline of plans for further development.

THE LEARNERS

Intake

The Study-Centre offers two categories of programme.

Referral programmes.   Students requiring supplementary tuition are identified by their regular English-class teachers during the first few weeks of the 'service' course and are referred to the Study-Centre in pairs or small groups. Referred students constitute roughly the lowest 20% of a class.

Each referral drive is followed by a compulsory twenty-hour programme of instruction. Groups are expected to attend twice weekly. A booking system is in operation in order that they may attend at their own convenience.

Summer programmes.   These are open to all Polytechnic students who would like to practise their English. Attendance is optional.

A learner-independent approach?

Sheerin (1989:3) states that the primary aim of self-access facilities is 'to enable learning to take place independently of teaching. Students are able to choose and use self-access material on their own. . . . students are able to direct their own learning'. It needs stressing perhaps that this should be viewed as the ultimate aim of a self-access centre, rather than as an objective which may be immediately realized. However, independent learning has successfully been achieved amongst a number of users in many centres by providing initial learner training programmes (Harding-Esch 1982; Riley and Zoppis 1985; Dickinson 1987; Sheerin 1992). Learners are thereby given assistance with the definition of learning aims, the identification of learning needs and with the selection of relevant materials. Subsequent, occasional, access to a counsellor is sufficient to enable a substantial number of learners to pursue their studies independently. At the same time, Riley (1987:77) stresses that 'the person responsible for setting up a self-access system should have a good, hard look at his prospective clients — their needs, objectives, interests, practical constraints and motivations . . . '

The majority of centres referred to above are in Western European countries in which one of the policies in education is to develop autonomy in the learning process. Initial investigations at Hong Kong Polytechnic indicate that this is not the case in Hong Kong where, certainly at secondary level, and in many cases at tertiary level, tuition is highly structured and where learners are expected to, and themselves expect to, adopt a highly passive role. Indeed, it might be said that formal education in this context teaches the need to be taught: learners are conditioned to believe that in order to learn one must be taught and that the teacher holds a monopoly over the transmission of knowledge.

Such a situation results in two major limitations:

1. Learners have no foundation on which to develop autonomy and many have difficulty in even accepting the notion of independent learning. Initially, many students attending the Study-Centre showed open resistance to the idea of assessing their own needs, planning their own programmes and selecting relevant materials. Many were bewildered by the idea of accepting responsibility for their learning. They continue to feel very strongly that the absence of a teacher is a laxity on our part.

2. Students lack confidence in using English. An analysis of the needs of students attending the Study-Centre indicates that the students' greatest perceived need is in the area of spoken English. However, students lack the confidence to participate in speaking activities without a very large measure of help and guidance from teachers; they need considerable direction and encouragement in working through activities and in maintaining momentum.

The expectations of learners in Hong Kong and a lack of self-reliance impose two sets of limitations on implementing an independent approach to language learning in Hong Kong. There are further limitations specific to the Study-Centre:

— The Centre caters to students who are particularly weak, some with a level of English little more than that of a post-beginner. These are learners who have already had little success in learning English and therefore require substantially more guidance and counselling.

— The programmes are compulsory. Initially, a number of students appear little motivated to learn English by any means, let alone independently.

— Students have to date been drawn from among the first-year intake to the Polytechnic. They have, therefore, had little opportunity to develop study skills within their own specialisms which might be transferred to a language-learning context.

— The programmes offered by the Centre are necessarily short. Given the large number of students for which the Centre caters, the programmes are restricted to twenty hours in length. Students expect to spend a very substantial amount of that time on language learning activities. If programmes are to have face validity, the amount of time that can be spent on learner training is extremely limited.

The utmost caution is required in introducing self-directed learning to these students. It should not be thrust upon learners who are not ready for it. As enthusiastic advocates we should not 'confuse the idea, or our enthusiasm to introduce it, with the learner's ability or willingness to undertake it' (Dickinson 1987:2). However, this is not to say that we should abandon all attempts to instil and foster independent learning. In these situations the way forward is to introduce into the learning programme elements which train learners towards greater autonomy and aim towards a gradual development to full autonomy (Dickinson 1987). Dickinson represents this gradual move towards greater learner autonomy as a continuum:

> very   full
> teacher- |_1_|_2_|_3_|_4_|_5_|_6_|_7_|_8_|_9_| autonomy
> directed
>   (after Dickinson 1987)

Different learners have differing starting points; it is therefore important to identify an appropriate starting point and begin at where the learners are, even if this means beginning at almost 'degree zero'. We need similarly to accept that different learners will advance at differing rates and have differing degrees of success. There is therefore a need to recognize and accept the limitations of our learners before embarking on a project aimed at introducing self-directed learning.

The Centre at Hong Kong Polytechnic has, therefore, adopted a 'shallow-end' approach to self-access, one which we hope will satisfy the students' perceived need for teacher contact while introducing students to the rudiments of learner independence and learner responsibility.

THE STUDY PROGRAMME: SEMESTER 1

A group orientated approach

In preparing learners for learner autonomy, it is important to take account of cultural variations (Riley 1988). Hong Kong appears to be a group-oriented society; consequently, the programmes are as far as possible group driven and group negotiated. This provides peer support, offers greater opportunities for communication, and thereby helps to increase confidence. Learners feel less exposed than they would if working individually or when called upon to perform in front of a large class. It should be noted that the term self-access has led perhaps, to too much of a focus on the individual to the exclusion of the group. As Dickinson and Carver (1980:3) have pointed out, 'Autonomous learning does not imply learning in isolation, and many aspects of language practice are best done with others'.

Programme structure

Session 1: group profile.   Groups have a short, informal talk with a teacher in the Centre. The purpose is to introduce the Centre, set students at ease, build up a rapport and provide an opportunity for them to voice their own concerns and interests.

Sessions 2–5: foundation component.   Groups work through a set menu of activities giving practice in a range of skills. This helps teachers identify more precisely the students' areas of weakness and enables students to make their own, informed choices as to the areas of language and skills which they need to practise later in the programme.

Session 6: needs assessment.   Groups have a short discussion with a teacher to identify the areas of the language in which they feel they need practice.

Sessions 7–20: core component.   This centres on those areas of difficulty which groups of students tend to have in common and takes account of weaknesses identified by class teachers as well as of students' own interests. Groups choose an area and activity type at the beginning of each session, based on those identified during the needs assessment. In session 15, groups are asked to complete a questionnaire in order to give their evaluation of the study programmes and the learning/teaching approaches.

After the programme had been running for some time forty-seven students (within one department of the Polytechnic) complained to their department that the Study Centre programmes were inadequate. A hastily conducted survey indicated that a significant number of other students were dissatisfied with the programme offered. Their grievances, among others, were that they were given inadequate teacher contact and supervision and that the programmes were unstructured.

In order to avoid a wholesale exodus of students, a much higher degree of guidance was immediately provided, with many groups receiving 100% teacher contact. At the same time, parts of the programme design were revised to provide a tighter structure.

THE STUDY PROGRAMME: SEMESTER 2

The following components were amended:

Session 6: needs assessment.   Groups complete an extensive needs analy-

sis questionnaire (Appendix 1) with guidance from a teacher. Part one of
the questionnaire asks groups to assess the importance of broad areas of
the language and rate these using a five-point scale; they then select three
or four areas which they would like to work on. Part two is more focused: groups are provided with a series of picklists from which they
choose specific language structures, functions, writing formats and topic
areas which they consider relevant. The group, with the aid of the completed needs questionnaire, and again guided by a teacher, draw up a
detailed and often extensive programme of study to include the specific
materials they will use (Appendix 2). The reaction of students has been
very positive: many have reported that close involvement at the planning
stage has led to a greater commitment to the programme and thereby to a
higher degree of motivation towards the learning of English.

Sessions 7–20: core component.   The programme invariably provides far
more material than the group will be able to cover in the time available.
The group selects from their programme at the start of each session.
Student choice therefore remains an integral part of the study programme.

At the end of each visit, groups are expected to complete a record of
work and provide a brief evaluation of the session (Appendix 3).

EVALUATION

A survey, in the form of a questionnaire, was conducted in April 1993
asking students to evaluate the study programmes, the teaching/learning
approaches, and their levels of confidence. The survey was made using a
questionnaire in the form of a five-point Likert scale,[1] with the categories
strongly agree, agree, neutral, disagree and strongly disagree; for the purposes of this discussion, these have been conflated to three: agree, neutral
and disagree. 171 students answered the questionnaire after completing
roughly three-quarters of their study programme. The responses relating
to learner independence can be seen in Table 1.

It should be stressed, firstly, that this is not a rigorous piece of research and any conclusions drawn must therefore be tentative. The discussion below suggests possible trends which emerge from an analysis of
the data.

Identification of needs and selection of materials.   The positive response
to the needs analysis is encouraging: a large proportion of students (62%)
appear not only to have recognized the value of analysing their own needs
but also feel that they have succeeded in the exercise. There is also a fairly

Table 1   Learner Independence in the Study-Centre

Item	Agree	Neutral	Disagree
Identification of needs and selection of materials			
The needs questionnaire in session 6 helped me decide which areas of the language I should practise.	62%	32%	6%
The study programme has given me practice in the areas which I consider important.	68%	31%	1%
I enjoy being able to choose which areas of the language to practise.	82%	16%	2%
The foundation programme (sessions 1–5) was a valuable introduction to the Centre.	35%	45%	20%
Independence from teachers			
It is important to have a teacher for the whole session when studying in the Centre.	80%	17%	3%
There is enough guidance from teachers in the Centre.	61%	34%	5%
I like having different teachers in different sessions.	61%	25%	14%
I feel better able to work on my own now since studying in the Centre.	31%	56%	13%

close match between those who felt that the questionnaire helped them initially to identify suitable areas and those who believed (68%) that the subsequent programme was relevant. Furthermore, few students appear to have reacted negatively.

There appears also to be a positive reaction (82%) to the self-selection of materials which formed an integral part of the 'Core Component'. In contrast, there was only limited enthusiasm for the 'Foundation Component' which offers little choice. There are, of course, many factors which could have influenced this reaction, but it is interesting to speculate whether this resulted from the lack of choice.

Independence from teachers.   Predictably, the majority of students (80%) believe that 100% teacher-contact is important but a large proportion (61%) feel that the amount of time spent with a teacher in the Centre (roughly 80% of a session) is acceptable and certainly few disagreed. A surprising number (61%) enjoyed the changeover of teachers from session to session. Students are therefore not dependent on a single teacher which suggests at least a small step in the direction of a more independent approach to learning. Overall, 31% of respondents felt that they had developed some independence, a figure which, though small, is encouraging.

CONCLUSION

It seems that the format of the study programmes offered to students does provide some, albeit very limited, opportunity to develop the basic elements of independence: students are given responsibility for determining their own needs, drawing up their own programmes and selecting relevant materials. Students have reacted positively to this shift in control. However, groups remain heavily dependant on teacher direction while working through activities. Although there is no reason why a self-access approach should preclude some teacher direction, it is desirable to limit intervention as far as possible without alienating the learner. Now that we have a programme structure offering a modicum of independence that appears acceptable to students, we should try (cautiously) to extend that autonomy. There are a number of possible developments which might address this issue.

1. A learner training package which may be used to supplement the 'Foundation' component is currently being piloted.
2. The programmes based on the present needs analysis give little overall direction and lack cohesion. As one student pointed out, 'It is not a systematic learning programme'. Students need training in the formulation of a set of objectives, perhaps embodied in a form of learner contract. They also need training in self-assessment.
3. Through further analysis of student evaluation, it may be possible to determine whether some categories of student need more direction than others. Different levels of direction could then be provided for the different categories.
4. Perhaps the Study-Centre should be regarded as a half-way house between a classroom-based approach and a more orthodox self-access mode. We are now planning to establish a 'self-study' area for use by students who have completed a regular study programme at the Centre. Students would have access to a full-time counsellor for guidance in the analysis of needs and the design of a further programme, but thereafter would be expected to work through activities with greater independence. The regular programme would thereby act as a vehicle leading to fuller autonomy and subsequent programmes would provide a measure of sustainability which at present is lacking.

Finally, we should be realistic as to how much independence our students can cope with initially — where on the continuum they should start — and how much autonomy we can expect of them within a limited programme of study. We need to recognize and respect the expectations of learners in Hong Kong and the needs and expectations specific to the target learners of particular institutions. We ignore these expectations at our peril.

NOTE

1. For a discussion of this form of evaluation see Oppenheim 1992:133–42.

REFERENCES

Blue, G.M. 1988. 'Self-assessment: the limits of learner independence', in A. Brookes and P. Grundy (eds.) *Individualization and Autonomy in Language Learning*. ELT Documents 131: The British Council.

Dickinson, L. 1987. *Self-instruction in Language Learning*. Cambridge: Cambridge University Press.

Dickinson, L. and Carver, D. 1980. 'Learning how to learn: steps towards self-direction in foreign language learning in schools'. *ELT Journal* 35(1):1–7.

Harding-Esch, E. 1982. 'The Open Access Sound and Video Library of the University of Cambridge: progress report and development'. *System* 10(1):13–28.

Oppenheim, A.N. 1992. *Questionnaire Design, Interviewing and Attitude Measurement*. Pinter Publishers.

Riley, P. 1987. 'From self-access to self-direction', in J.A. Coleman and R. Towell (eds.) *The Advanced Language Learner*. London: CILT.

———. 1988. 'The ethnography of autonomy', in A. Brookes and P. Grundy (eds.) *Individualization and Autonomy in Language Learning*. ELT Documents 131: The British Council.

Riley, P. and Zoppis, C. 1985. 'The Sound and Video Library', in P. Riley (ed.) *Discourse and Learning*. Harlow, Essex: Longman.

Sheerin, S. 1989. *Self-Access*. Oxford: Oxford University Press.

———. 1991. 'Self-access'. *Language Teaching* 24(3):143–57.

APPENDIX 1

Your Learning Needs

Group: **Course:**

The purpose of this questionnaire is to help you decide which language areas you would like to practise.

Part A*

1. For each area listed, ask yourself how necessary or important it is for you and circle one of the numbers (1 = least important; 5 = most important).

	Language Area	*How necessary is it?*
1	**Listening**	least most
1.1	Conversational (social English)	1 2 3 4 5
1.2	Academic (e.g. lectures, taking notes)	1 2 3 4 5
1.3	Listening for pleasure (e.g. radio, film)	1 2 3 4 5
2	**Speaking**	
2.1	Conversational (social English)	1 2 3 4 5
2.2	Academic (e.g. oral presentations)	1 2 3 4 5
3	**Reading**	
3.1	Increasing speed	1 2 3 4 5
3.2	Improving comprehension	1 2 3 4 5
3.3	Note-taking	1 2 3 4 5
3.4	Related to specialism	1 2 3 4 5
3.5	Reading for pleasure	1 2 3 4 5
4	**Writing**	
4.1	Personal (e.g. letters to friends)	1 2 3 4 5
4.2	Formal (e.g. reports, business letters)	1 2 3 4 5
4.3	Organisation of ideas (e.g. linkwords, punctuation)	1 2 3 4 5
5	**Vocabulary**	1 2 3 4 5
6	**Pronunciation**	
6.1	Individual sounds	1 2 3 4 5
6.2	Stress and intonation	1 2 3 4 5
7	**Grammar**	1 2 3 4 5

---

* Part A is adapted from G.M. Blue (1988)

2. Look again at the questionnaire and list the three or four activities you would most like to practise:

    1. _____

    2. _____

    3. _____

    4. _____

Part B

Refer to the lists which the teacher will give you.

1. Are there any grammatical areas you would like to practise?

    _____

    _____

    _____

    _____

2. Are there any functions that you would like to practise?

    _____

    _____

    _____

    _____

3. Are there any topic areas which interest you?

    _____

    _____

    _____

    _____

    Which would you prefer:
    a. *some* of the materials to be related to your own degree subject; or
    b. *all* materials related to general topics (as in the foundation programme)?

    _____

4. Are there any particular types of writing you would like to practise?

    _____

    _____

    _____

    _____

5. Any other requests?

    _____

    _____

    _____

    _____

PICKLISTS FOR NEEDS ANALYSIS

1. Grammatical Areas

Tenses
past simple, past continuous

present simple, present continuous

present perfect simple (with for and since)

future

passives

reported speech

Miscellaneous
articles a, an and the

relative clauses

comparatives and superlatives (for example: taller, tallest)

conditionals (If clauses)

conjunctions (for example: and, but, so . . . .)

countable/uncountable nouns, how much/how many

gerunds (nouns with ing)

infinitives (to + verb)

phrasal verbs

prepositions

punctuation

questions – direct/indirect questions
'wh. . .' questions
yes and no questions

word order

2. Functions

Information, opinions and ideas
agreeing and disagreeing

giving reasons

comparing

complaining

describing experiences

describing objects

describing people

describing places

describing processes

instructions/directions

likes and dislikes/preferences

obligation (for example: have to, must, should, ought to)

opinions

possibility, probability (for example: could, may, might, will)

Social Conventions
(for example: apologizing, forgiving, complimenting, congratulating, introduction and greetings, saying goodbye, thanking)

Telling/Asking To Do Things
invitations

offers

orders, commands

permission

persuading

requests

suggestions and advice

3. Topics

advertising
animals
art
biography
business
clothing
law and crime
disaster
customs/festivals
education
employment
entertainment
environment
family and friends
food and drink
future
medicine/health/illness
history
hobbies

holidays
housing/accommodation
marriage
media
war
money
politics and government
religion
science
shopping
social issues (for example: poverty, old age)
sports
supernatural and superstitions
technology
transport
travel/different cultures
weather/climate

4. Writing

curriculum vitae
essays
form-filling
instructions
letters (informal)
letters (business)

memos
notices
speeches
stories
summaries

APPENDIX 2

Study Programme

Group: ABCT/9
Date: 16 March 1993

A wide range of interests emerged from our discussion: it may not be possible to complete the entire programme in the time available.

Skill	Focus	Pathways/Coursebooks	Hours	√
Speaking	- Social English	- 'In at the Deep End' U16	1 hr	☐
	- Dangerous sports	- 'The Last Word' U10	1 hr	☐
	- Sports	- 'Speaking Intermediate' U3	1 hr	☐
	- Oral presentations	- ELSC Presentation Packs (textiles-related)	2 hrs+	☐
Functions		- *complaining (I)*	2 hrs	☐
		- *comparing (I)*	2 hrs	☐
Grammar		- reported speech (I)	2 hrs	☐
		- prepositions (I)	2 hrs	☐
		- gerunds and infinitives (I)	2 hrs	☐
		- *conditionals (I)*	2 hrs	☐
Listening	- advertising/complaints	- 'Play it by ear' U8	1 hr	☐
	- sports	- 'Soundings' U5	1 hr	☐
Reading	- Newspaper articles	- See index		
Writing	- Reports	- 'Perspectives' U12	1–2 hrs	☐
	- Job applications	- 'Writing Matters' U11 [NB. you need a copy of the Morning Post for Exercise 7]	2 hrs	☐
Vocabulary	- Phrasal verbs	- 'Build your Vocabulary' U14	¼ hr	☐
	- Phrasal verbs	- 'Build your Vocabulary' U24	¼ hr	☐
		- 'Build your Vocabulary' U41	¼ hr	☐

APPENDIX 3

English Language Study-Centre: Record of Work

Session	Task/Learning Pathways	Evaluation How valuable did you find this session?	Comments	Dates
1		Very Not at all 1 2 3 4 5 →		
2		Very Not at all 1 2 3 4 5 →		
3		Very Not at all 1 2 3 4 5 →		
4		Very Not at all 1 2 3 4 5 →		
5		Very Not at all 1 2 3 4 5 →		
6		Very Not at all 1 2 3 4 5 →		
7		Very Not at all 1 2 3 4 5 →		
8		Very Not at all 1 2 3 4 5 →		
9		Very Not at all 1 2 3 4 5 →		
10		Very Not at all 1 2 3 4 5 →		
11		Very Not at all 1 2 3 4 5 →		
12		Very Not at all 1 2 3 4 5 →		
13		Very Not at all 1 2 3 4 5 →		
14		Very Not at all 1 2 3 4 5 →		
15		Very Not at all 1 2 3 4 5 →		
16		Very Not at all 1 2 3 4 5 →		
17		Very Not at all 1 2 3 4 5 →		
18		Very Not at all 1 2 3 4 5 →		
19		Very Not at all 1 2 3 4 5 →		
20		Very Not at all 1 2 3 4 5 →		

CHAPTER 3

A Self-Directed Project: A Critical Humanistic Approach to Self-Access

Terence T.T. Pang, Lingnan College, Hong Kong

INTRODUCTION

A centrally administered special fund has been established in Hong Kong to provide grants for language enhancement. This Language Enhancement Grant has provided an unprecedented opportunity for working towards the ideals of equal access in language development for all tertiary students in Hong Kong. This is necessitated by the rapid expansion of tertiary education in recent years in the territory. The facilities that can be developed by using the Language Enhancement Grant ensure that students will be able to complete their tertiary education successfully, without being handicapped by language problems. They also ensure quality of education in addition to quantity of places in tertiary institutes; language enhancement is a necessity rather than a luxury. The provision of the Language Enhancement Grant has created vast opportunities for the utilization of human and physical resources in the area of self-directed language learning.

The paradigm underpinning the self-directed project at Lingnan College originates from two main theoretical perspectives: the first in education and psychology encompasses the Critical Humanistic Educational Administration School (Kemmis 1985), self-directed learning (Bella-Dora and Blanchard 1979), co-operative learning (Bossert 1989), learning style (Hill 1976) and personal construct theory (Riley 1985); and the second in discourse encompassing the situational analysis of Hymes (1977), the functional grammar and social semiotics of Halliday (1978), and genre analysis (Martin 1984; Swales 1990).

The approach outlined here is based on the humanistic concept of the learner as a sensible and sane human being who is capable of learning language in a realistic context through interaction and learning with and from peers, and making sensible decisions along the way. The programme addresses the vital issues of learner independence, learning style, learner training, self-direction and collaborative learning in a non-threatening environment. It stresses the importance of critical self-reflection to the extent that it can be said that learners are in fact engaged in heuristic action research on their own learning while learning the language in a self-directed mode.

The approach is critical in that both the learner and the teacher are constantly involved in the discourses of negotiation and contention as well as qualitative evaluation through reflection on the learning process. It is humanistic in that the primary focus is on the learner. The culture, the interests, the interlanguage and the idiolect of the learners become the most valuable resources of the self-access centre (SAC). In this approach, which is underpinned by the concept of genre, language is regarded as an evolving cultural artefact and linguistic maturity is viewed as the ability to use different voices for different occasions. Language use is regarded as an art rather than merely a skill, and hence there is no end to the search for perfection. Linguistic input is considered to be derived from the totality of learning experience of the learner, both inside and outside the SAC, linguistic and otherwise.

OBJECTIVES

The self-directed project at Lingnan College aims at helping learners develop independence and self-guidance in language learning. It moves in the direction of enabling learners to:
1. review their own language proficiency;
2. analyse their own language needs;
3. understand their own learning style;
4. have the opportunity to work with their peers;
5. learn from each other, decision-making processes and language learning and language use;
6. critically examine the use of language in the real world,
7. use English for self-reflection;
8. use English in a real world context;
9. use language for worthwhile and ethically justifiable causes;
10. gain access to hitherto unfamiliar discourse communities;
11. acquire genre(s) realistically;
12. present their work appropriately;
13. evaluate their experience in implementing project-based work;
14. assess their future language needs realistically; and
15. plan their future language learning strategies accordingly.

THE PROGRAMME

The Lingnan programme is self-directed, project-based and task-based and involves learning both inside and outside the SAC (Fig. 1). The learners are first-year students who have scored above E in the Use of English and hence are not eligible for the otherwise compulsory English Foundation Course which is also funded by the Language Enhancement

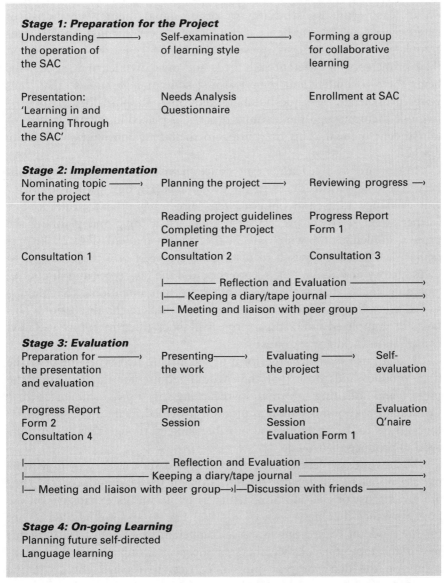

Stage 1: Preparation for the Project

| Understanding ⟶ the operation of the SAC | Self-examination ⟶ of learning style | Forming a group for collaborative learning |

| Presentation: 'Learning in and Learning Through the SAC' | Needs Analysis Questionnaire | Enrollment at SAC |

Stage 2: Implementation

Nominating topic ⟶ for the project   Planning the project ⟶   Reviewing progress ⟶

| Consultation 1 | Reading project guidelines Completing the Project Planner Consultation 2 | Progress Report Form 1 Consultation 3 |

⊢————— Reflection and Evaluation —————⟶
⊢—— Keeping a diary/tape journal —————⟶
⊢— Meeting and liaison with peer group —————⟶

Stage 3: Evaluation

Preparation for ⟶ the presentation and evaluation   Presenting⟶ the work   Evaluating ⟶ the project   Self-evaluation

| Progress Report Form 2 Consultation 4 | Presentation Session | Evaluation Session Evaluation Form 1 | Evaluation Q'naire |

⊢————————— Reflection and Evaluation —————⟶
⊢————————— Keeping a diary/tape journal —————⟶
⊢— Meeting and liaison with peer group—⟶⊢—Discussion with friends —————⟶

Stage 4: On-going Learning
Planning future self-directed
Language learning

Figure 1   The Stages of the Project-based Collaborative Learning at the SAC

Grant. Previous experience shows that many students who were excluded from the foundation course felt that they also needed help with their English.

Before coming to the self-access centre, students attend a presentation called 'Learning In and Learning Through the SAC' which explains the operation of the centre and briefly introduces the self-directed programme.

To enrol in the course, learners sign up and receive a handbook which guides them through the course. The sign up procedure groups students into fives. They are advised to join groups with people unknown to them, or at least students studying in other departments. This ensures heterogenous groups and hence is conducive to peer learning. Each learner completes a needs analysis questionnaire of 75 questions reporting on their proficiency in different skill areas and their own learning style. This helps them to understand their learning style and to analyse their language proficiency. The questionnaire, like other support documents used to guide them through the learning process, is placed in the appendices of the student manual. This they bring to their first consultation with the teacher.

In Consultation 1, learners introduce themselves to their group members. The teacher introduces to the group a peer group with whom they will exchange ideas and opinions regarding each other's projects. The learners then start the process of nominating a topic and planning the project, guidelines for which are in the student manual (Fig. 2). In particular, learners are advised to distinguish between two project types — investigatory and activity-based projects, and the task types and discourse, including genre, that accompany each type. It is intentional that the assigned consultation time is not enough to complete the discussion. This must be completed later and a project planner filled in before the next consultation (held a week later).

A literature search, in the form of identifying text-types for both the final product and those that they would require for implementing the project and soliciting information regarding the topic, commences after Consultation 1. Some sample topics are provided in the manual (Fig. 3) for learners to derive an idea on possible choices, though they are encouraged to produce their own.

Meanwhile, the learners are encouraged to start a diary or tape journal as an instrument for critical reflection on the learning process. They are given a list of cue questions which is by no means exhaustive on the possible issues they may wish to address (Fig. 4) and are advised to opt for the mode of record they are less competent in, for most learners this means the tape journal. Members of the peer group record their comments on the diary or tape journal entries. Issues brought up in the learners' reflections are discussed in consultation sessions. The diary or

Identify a project which your group can manage to complete in ten weeks' time. The ten week period will commence immediately after Consultation 2 in which you will present your project proposal as outlined in the **project planner** in Appendix II. When you select a topic for your project, consider the following factors:

1. **Your interest** — You are more likely to implement a project which suits the interest of all group members.

2. **Your knowledge** — Rather than selecting a topic which you know a lot about, select one that you have to explore, by way of both literature search at the beginning, and action during the implementation. This way, both your knowledge and your language will be enriched.

3. **Your language** — Try to venture into a field and a task type that would require you to come into touch with and use language that you are not very familiar with.

4. **Learning style** — Select a topic that would suit your learning style. You can discover your learning style by reviewing the questions in sections D and E of the Needs Analysis Questionnaire (Appendix I). Simply put, learning style is the totality of your study habits and the approach(es) you adopt to solve problems and to make decisions.

5. **Task type** — Select a topic with a task type that is not so familiar to you. Basically, projects can be classified as either **investigatory** which would engage you in some fact-finding tasks, or **activity-based**, which will engage you in some sort of real life activity. The language used in both also differ.

Figure 2   Project Guidelines

1. Staging a performance in an elderly home or an orphanage.

2. Assessing the entertainment needs of children with Down's Syndrome.

3. Giving talks to secondary children on topics like drug abuse, summer vacation activities.

4. Organizing an essay/speaking competition for the students in Lingnan Middle School.

5. Organizing a visit to an English School Foundation/International School.

6. Compiling a cultural activities list for the coming month in Hong Kong.

7. Writing a report on the recreational activities of Filipino domestic helpers in Hong Kong.

8. Organizing an inter-college debate with the Baptist College and Shue Yan College Student Unions.

Figure 3   Sample Topics

Here is a list of questions that you may consider as cues to respond to while you are composing your diary or tape journal entries.

1. Why are you working on the project? Is it simply a course requirement, or is it for learning a language, or is it for learning how to learn?
2. How well planned is the project? Do you need to make any changes and modifications?
3. Where can you have access to information and resources regarding your project? Have you encountered any difficulties in doing so?
4. How are you processing/did you process the information collected?
5. How are you going to/did you utilize the information?
6. How are you working with/going to work with your partners? Do you want to work individually, in a pair or in a group?
7. How are you going to arrange your time for your project? Have you got a schedule which includes all your other commitments? How many hours do you need in order to complete the project?
8. Where are you going to work — at home, in the SAC, in the College Library or in the canteen?
9. What are the tasks involved in the project?
10. What kind of language and text types do you need to know in order to complete the various tasks in the project?
11. Where are you going to get assistance in case you have difficulty(ies) with the language demands of the tasks?
12. What do you feel about composing this diary/tape journal?
13. How well have you enjoyed working on your project so far?
14. How well have you been working with your partners so far?
15. Have you learned anything from working with your partners?
16. Have you discovered anything about the way you approach problems that you did not realize before?
17. Have you learned any 'new language' while working on this project?
18. How do you feel about working with relatively little teacher guidance?
19. If you had a chance to start again, would you have conducted the work you have done so far in a different way?
20. Do you think you are more confident to work independently and/or with your friends as a result of working on this project?

Figure 4   Cue Questions for Diary/Tape Journal

tape journal also provides a record for critical evaluation of the entire learning experience at the end of the project.

Three consultation sessions follow the first one at intervals of about two to three weeks, each reviews progress with the aid of a progress review form designed specifically for the purpose. The final consultation session focuses on preparation for the end-of-project presentation and evaluation session. Between consultation sessions, the teacher is available for advice on project related issues. In consultation learners are encouraged to seek their own solutions to their problems.

The presentation is assessed by the peer group, who should by this stage be familiar with the other group's project through reviewing their diaries/tape journals and meetings. They should be able to appreciate the difficulties encountered and the efforts made and thus give realistic assessment of the presenters' achievement. This qualitative assessment is facilitated by the provision of an evaluation form in the student manual. This requires evaluators to examine first the positive aspects of the project work. Secondly, any shortcomings are in the form of recommendations for future action which are then discussed in a meeting held between the two groups before coming to the evaluation session.

After the two groups have assessed each other's projects and presentation, they join in an evaluation session, sharing their experience and planning their future language learning strategies. Any opinions arising from the discussion on the projects and final products can be recorded on the evaluation form. The learners also answer an evaluation questionnaire in the appendix of the manual after reviewing their diary or tape journal, and complete a future self-directed language learning planner. They are also encouraged to continue keeping the diary or tape journal and to exchange language learning tips with their friends.

THE ROLE OF THE SAC

The approach proposed here addresses the concern of some ESL/EFL teachers who are not entirely converted to the idea of self-access language learning (SALL). Typically, they believe that the kind of SALL activities that takes place exclusively in a practice laboratory are other-directed rather than self-directed (Pennycook 1993); that the mode of learning is mechanistic, with learners interacting with technology rather than interacting with humans (a revised form of audiolingualism); and that the discourse learners acquire is not authentic, real world discourse.

The approach outlined above may appear to some traditional self-access practitioners to reduce the role of the SAC. However, priorities must be clear. It is the learners rather than the centre as a physical resource that we should focus on. Moreover, by promoting the idea that the SAC is a physical resource instead of an activity-based entity, we are actually diminishing the role of the SAC and not fully exploiting its potential. In the situation described here, the SAC acts to provide much needed consultation and support — moral, pedagogical, linguistic and tactical. It acts as a resource base to which learners can turn in search of materials to overcome problems they encounter with language and discourse. It is a possible venue where they can obtain generic samples for the real world tasks with which they have to cope while working on the project or producing the final presentation. They can also obtain advice in the SAC for handling an unfamiliar verbal genre — the presentation. Placing student generated products in a wide range of media forms in the

SAC also renders an invaluable service as a museum of veritable artifacts which can be used as language learning materials as well as reference samples for future project planners.

If learning in the SAC as in all other settings occurs in a cline between self-directed and other-directed, then the approach advocated here is obviously closer to the former. The contribution of the teacher is found in the design of the overall shape of the learning experience, but the project type, the accompanying task and hence discourse types are chosen by the learners who also take responsibility for organizing the work, managing their schedule and time, evaluating the learning experience, assessing the final product and planning their future learning. The teacher's role is that of an equal, a facilitator. The power relationships between teacher and learner and among learners themselves are democratic. The teacher does not abstain from giving advice, but does not put the learner in a dependent position.

PROGRAMME EVALUATION

The critical humanistic approach adopted by the self-directed project reported on here renders action research the most appropriate instrument of course evaluation.

This kind of action research tends to be subjective because the researcher is also the evaluator. However, it is expected that the researcher will accept both surprises and constructive criticisms, from the institution, colleague and learners, and from the research itself. Action research is appropriate in this context because the participants would like to see the practice improved through critical self-evaluation. There are two groups of participants in the self-directed learning programme — the learners wishing to improve their language proficiency, their learning strategies and to modify their learning styles; and the teacher interested in improving the organization of the programme.

The educational nature of action research makes it too valuable as a tool to be denied to the learners. By constantly reflecting on their own learning and recording the results of such reflections in their progress review forms and the evaluation documents as well as in their diary/tape journal, the learners are engaged in action research. As a pathway to improve practice, student initiated action research is directly relevant to self-directed learning. Action research consisting of identification of a 'problem' or the general idea, reconnaissance, planning, action steps, monitoring, further reconnaissance and revision of the general idea, is particularly relevant to the self-directed project model described in this paper. The learners' objectives in action research, implied in the instructional design, and made known to them right from the beginning, are three-fold — learning about self, learning about learning (a language) and learning to learn. The ability to reflect and to participate in critical debate is facilitated by peer evaluation in the forms of commenting on other learners' diaries/tape journals, and of participating in peer group meetings, though the value of these tools has yet to be established. Their feedback, in both their self-evaluation and their comments on the 'instructional design', constitutes the most valuable data for the teacher's action research. In this sense at least, the action research is collaborative. Other instruments for generating data consist of: recordings of consultation sessions; teacher diary; and interviews and consultations with individual students.

CONCLUSION

Several promises and claims have been made regarding the value and potential of this project. It is only through action and research in action, that such claims can be verified. The validity of the claims which would justify the feasibility of the programme ultimately rests with the consensus of all the participants, in this case the institution, the teacher(s) and above all, the learners.

The programme is a reaction and a challenge to the technocratic influences that permeate education in general and the ELT profession in particular. As such, potential difficulties cannot be easily predicted. To start with, learner acceptance of self-directed learning is an unknown factor, even though the programme still contains a certain degree of teacher and peer-direction. The group monitor effect in co-operative learning may help overcome the culture shock accompanying a shift towards self-directed learning, but may prove counter-productive in affective terms. The ultimate fate of the project may well hinge on how participants employ the skills which they acquire and pass the word to other students as to the effectiveness of such a programme.

REFERENCES

Bossert, S. 1988–89. 'Co-operative activities in the classroom', in E.Z. Rothkopf (ed.) *Review of Research in Education, Volume 15.* Itasca, IL: F.E. Peacock Publishers

Bella-Dora, D. and Blanchard, L.J. 1979. *Moving Toward Self-Directed Learning: Highlights of Relevant Research and of Promising Practices.* Alexandria, VA: ASCD.

Halliday, M.A.K. 1978. *Language as Social Semiotic: The Social Interpretation of Language and Meaning*. London: Edward Arnold.

Hill, J.B. 1976. *The Educational Sciences*. Bloomfield, ML: Oakland Community College.

Hymes, D. 1977. *Foundations in Sociolinguistics: An Ethnographic Approach*. London: Tavistock Publications.

Kemmis, S. 1985. 'Action research and the politics of reflection', in D. Bond, R. Keogh and D. Walke (eds.) *Reflection: Turning Experience into Learning*. London: Kogan Page.

Martin, J. 1984. 'Language, register and genre', in *Language Studies: Children Writing Leader*. 1987 Geelong: Deakin University Press.

Pennycook, A. 1993. 'Some thoughts on self-access'. *Self-Access UPDATE for Teachers* 3:3. English Centre, The University of Hong Kong.

Riley, P. 1985. 'Mud and stars: personal constructs, sensitization and learning', in P. Riley (ed.) *Discourse and Learning*. London: Longman.

Swales, J.M. 1990. *Genre Analysis: English in Academic and Research Settings*. Cambridge: Cambridge University Press.

CHAPTER 4

Self-Access Writing Centres

Kathy Hayward, English Language Teaching Unit,
The Chinese University of Hong Kong

INTRODUCTION

Writing is the most prized of academic skills. It is by writing that most students studying at tertiary level are assessed and pass or fail their courses. Many native English users find writing difficult, so how much more difficult is it for non-native users of the language? This paper looks at the development of writing centres as part of self access centres (SAC) in the drive towards helping non-native English users with their writing.

THE BAPTIST COLLEGE EXPERIENCE

In Hong Kong we have seen an increase in tertiary education and an increase in the number of students who have problems with expressing themselves through written English. This was a concern to the teaching staff at Baptist College, particularly from the Arts and Social Science faculties, who noted that despite a first-year course in English for Academic Purposes, which concentrated on writing skills, many students experienced great difficulties with writing their term papers and honours projects in their second and third years. When Baptist College received the grant earmarked for language enhancement, it was decided to spend one-third of the money on a writing centre. This writing centre, called the Writing Enhancement Service, has now been running for two years. It employs four full-time tutors, three for English and one for Chinese. The Service is completely voluntary for the students and gives priority to those working on specific assignments in their major subjects. It does not help students who are writing assignments for their language courses. The tutors in the Baptist College writing centre help students with all aspects of the writing process, from narrowing a topic and writing an outline, to checking the final draft for errors. Aspects of the process that are concentrated on include organising and relating ideas, expressing those ideas clearly and concisely, and using outside sources correctly. Students are encouraged to come early on in the writing process.

Some of the principal benefits of the writing centre in the Baptist College have proved to be the following:
— the writing problems of each individual can receive more direct attention;
— the writing centre can help students with different aspects of the writing process at different times;
— the writing centre provides the only organized means of helping students with actual writing assignments in their major subjects;
— the writing centre is able to work with students at the very time they are motivated to seek help with their writing.

Although the writing centre has been successful on the whole, there have been some problems, arising mainly from misconceptions about the role of the centre:
— some students regard it as a proofreading service;
— some students see it as a course of private lessons;
— some students come with other needs — such as listening, reading, or oral English — because there seemed nowhere else for them to go;
— a related problem is that some members of staff tend to look upon the Writing Centre as a dumping ground for students generally weak in English.

THE INDEPENDENT LEARNING CENTRE AT THE CHINESE UNIVERSITY

The approach to helping learners with their writing problems at the Chinese University's Independent Learning Centre (ILC) is different from that outlined for the Baptist College. It was decided to establish a writing centre within the ILC itself. There are benefits to both the Writing Centre and the ILC with this approach.

Benefits to the Writing Centre

It saves tutorial time if the students can be encouraged to use the facilities in the ILC for much of the help they need. For example, the writing section in the ILC will contain models of types of writing the students can look through, including business letters, reports, and term papers. If they need to work on an area of grammar, they can be shown how to make use of the grammar sections and relevant CALL programs. Or they may find the reading section useful. In any case, all of these will be housed in the ILC, where the tutor can show students the relevant materials. This will help to train students to be independent and in those areas where they can work alone they will be encouraged to do so.

Some of the other benefits are directly related to the problems experienced in the writing centre at Baptist College: the tendency for some students to see the Writing Centre either as a proofreading service or as a course. That the Writing Centre is housed inside the ILC and identified with the ideology of independent learning will help the students see the tutors not as teachers who correct their work but as people who help them to help themselves. It will also help the tutors to define their role.

Students who show up at the Writing Centre with very general weaknesses in English, or who have needs in addition to writing, can be directed on the spot to counsellors and relevant materials in the ILC.

Benefits to the Independent Learning Centre

The inclusion of the Writing Centre in the ILC expands the range of options for the counsellor, who can now either help learners with writing problems or refer them to the writing centre for more extensive help.

The Writing Centre contributes materials to the writing section of the ILC. Being in the Writing Centre gives the tutors the opportunity to know which type of assignments the students are set, the kinds of problems they have and the type of activities that help students with their writing. They are able to produce handouts for the students that are of direct use. Anything that is produced to help students in the Writing Centre is also available in the writing section of the ILC.

By having the Writing Centre in the ILC, students become aware that we recognize that they have specific academic needs for English, which the ILC is attempting to meet. It strengthens the relevance of English to the whole enterprise of university education.

The Writing Centre attracts students into the ILC who would not ordinarily come: those who want to concentrate only on their major subjects and to improve the standard of their essays. Being in the ILC and being shown materials there, however, may encourage these students to work on other areas of English as well.

Finally, the presence of the Writing Centre in the ILC encourages the interest and involvement by staff in other departments. Teaching staff at Chinese University have already shown great interest in the setting up of a writing centre; and if they can be shown that the ILC is of direct tangible benefit to their students, it will get the support it needs from other departments to ensure its success.

CONCLUSION

I have described two approaches to meeting the writing needs of learners in an independent learning environment. The Writing Enhancement Service at Baptist College was a first attempt and it offers several benefits to the students which were not there before. However, the integration of a writing centre into the ILC at the Chinese University offers even greater scope to assist students become more proficient in writing in English.

Section Two

Learner Training

CHAPTER 5

Helping Learners Plan and Prepare for Self-Access Learning

Winnie W.F. Or, Language Centre, Hong Kong University of Science and Technology

INTRODUCTION

This paper reports on the planning and preparation stage of a self-access project undertaken by first year undergraduates at the Hong Kong University of Science and Technology (HKUST). It also discusses ways teachers can help learners build better learning paths and emphasizes the importance of teacher intervention in the planning and preparation stage, particularly in helping learners establish statements of objective, and analysing them. If we can help learners establish realistic and achievable goals, we can solve a lot of problems that might occur in the later stages of a self-instruction programme.

PROJECT OUTLINE

The project ran for 15 weeks during which students spent one hour per week working within a predetermined schedule (Table 1) on whichever area of language learning they chose.

Table 1   Outline of the Project

Weeks 1–3 Planning and Preparation	-induction to self-access learning -needs analysis -statement of objective -action plan -learner contract
Weeks 4–14 Activities	-selection of materials -learning activities -evaluation-tutorial presentation
Week 15 Assessment & Evaluation	-oral presentation -written report

INDUCTION AND NEEDS ANALYSIS

The first stage of the project began with a general induction to self-access learning. It took the form of a quiz, followed by a discussion of the answers (Appendix 1). After that, learners were given a General Needs Analysis questionnaire (Appendix 2). Section C, which is the main body of the needs analysis, consists of all the language focuses or skill areas and their sub-areas found in the cataloguing system of the self-access centre.

After completing the needs analysis and identifying the skill area that they would like to work on, those learners with the same area were put into one group, where they briefly described to each other their language learning experience and their problems, specifically those related to the area they had identified.

STATEMENTS OF OBJECTIVES

The learners were asked to write short statements describing the objectives of their learning programmes or projects. The following are examples collected from the learners:

1. *My goal is to improve the speed of listening and know how to catch the main ideas, so that I can follow the radio news, TV programmes, movies and lectures. It is also easier for me to take notes during lectures.*
2. *I choose social speaking as my self-access project. I want to improve my pronunciation and vocabulary.*
3. *In this project, I choose reading and my main goal is to improve my reading speed because reading faster can benefit my academic learning. By reading different materials, like magazines, newspapers and academic articles, I want to learn how to skim and scan to improve my reading speed.*
4. *I intend to improve my knowledge of preposition.*
5. *In this project, I want to improve the grammar and organisation of writing. Moreover, I hope to learn more vocabulary as well as increase the writing speed.*
6. *I will learn to write in fifteen weeks and I have two main sub-goals: they are organization and grammar.*

The statements of objective, messy though they may look, contain a lot of valuable information about the learners which we need to take into consideration when helping learners form a plan of action. Most of the statements of objective could not be used immediately as the basis for an action plan, but they do reflect a lot about the learners' beliefs, attitudes and motivation which are all variables that affect language learning. The following analysis of the above examples illustrates these points.

Statement 1: Lacks specificity of purpose. The learner wishes to improve his general listening ability for various purposes, for example, entertainment and academic study. It seems that he is not totally aware of the scope of the statement he makes (given that the project is only to last fifteen weeks). Or maybe he is not aware that different types of listening activity require different sets of sub-skills.

Statement 2: The learner seems to suggest that by improving her pronunciation and vocabulary, she would be able to improve her 'social speaking'. The term 'vocabulary', in this case, needs clarification. By 'vocabulary', the learner may be referring to specific topic-dependent lexical items, or more probably, in the case of social speaking, formulaic patterns of speech to serve an immediate communicative purpose when a conversation occurs. The reference to 'pronunciation', which is a segmental element, to improve speech also warrants some attention. Experience shows us that Hong Kong learners have as many, if not more, problems with supra-segmental elements of speech such as intonation.

Statement 3: This shares something in common with statements 1 and 4, in that the learners indicate their wish to increase 'speed', which they believe is important in a variety of listening, reading or writing tasks. In general, learners do not seem to realize that speed is only an indication of how efficient and effective they are in applying various sub-skills such as skimming and scanning in reading, and that it is not a skill in itself which one can practise. Very often, when learners indicate the need for enhancing speed, they resort to the strategy of repetition (as it is generally believed that practice makes perfect), which might not be very productive.

Statement 4: This is very discrete linguistically, so much so that the learner can start drawing up his action plan immediately. However, there is no attempt to contextualize the need and there is no clue as to why he wants to improve in this area. As the self-access project was compulsory and formed part of the assessment of the language enhancement course, the learner might have chosen such a focused topic because it seemed easy to complete rather than because it was an area in which he genuinely needed to improve.

Statement 5: The learner identifies the three main areas which she wants to work on to improve her writing, namely grammar, organization and vocabulary. It is not clear if the learner is aware of the complexity of writing proficiency, which also includes sociolinguistic competence (including style and register) and discourse competence (coherence and cohesion). The reason why the learner specifically identifies grammar, organization and vocabulary as areas requiring improvement may be that these terms are more familiar to her. 'Organizational errors' for many learners, is a catch-all term for anything other than 'grammatical mistakes' in writing.

Statement 6: This presents a very long-term goal, which is unrealistic in our case, and learners need to be made aware of this. Similar to statement 5, the learner seems to be suggesting that good writing means good organization and accurate grammar. The teacher may need to ask the learner to clarify what he means by 'organization', and through discussion, introduce textual and discoursal matters that need to be attended to in writing.

The statements of objective need to be examined and analyzed carefully, and to do this, there are at least three important aspects that we need to consider. They are expressed here in the form of a continuum (Fig. 1).

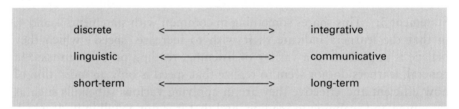

Figure 1   Continua for Measuring Statements of Objective

The extreme left of the continua indicates simplicity whereas the extreme right indicates complexity. Statement 4 on improving pronunciation, for example, would appear very much to the left of the continua, which indicates a rather simplistic goal. In such a case, we would need to ask the learner to contextualize the objective. For complex objectives, we should look for ways of helping students break them down into more manageable and operational sub-goals. The following is an example in which the learner's aim was to improve his 'speaking during tutorials'. His speaking ability was demonstrated to be at a poor level. When asked what he had been doing, he reported that he had been doing pronunciation practice in the language laboratory, but it seemed that the practice had got him nowhere.

In the consultation session, the learner was asked to brainstorm what he needed to do in tutorials, and he came up with:

— make a point,
— make an argument, and
— respond to an argument.

With some probing, he also pointed out that he needed to produce sentences, which are made up of words, which in turn are made up of phonemes. The ideas were presented to him in a table (Table 2) where his perceived needs (left) are matched against discrete language items. The learner realized by looking at the list what 'speaking in tutorials' really entails and that he could choose any of the items on the right to make them sub-goals of his study programme.

Table 2   Speaking in Tutorials

* responding to an argument	* listening and understanding * inferencing
* making an argument	* organization of ideas * signposts and discourse markers
* making a point with several sentences	* knowledge of the subject (reading) * cohesive devices
* sentences	* intonation * rhythm * neutralization of weak forms * elision * grammar
* words	* word stress elision
* phonemes	* consonants * vowels * diphthongs

Besides helping learners break down their objectives into manageable and operational sub-goals, the tutor can help the learners understand what strategies are available to tackle those goals. However, some strategies may not be within the learner's repertoire, which, if too limited, may need expansion.

CONCLUSION

The above discussion of the planning and preparation stage of a self-access programme can best be summarized in a model (Fig. 2).

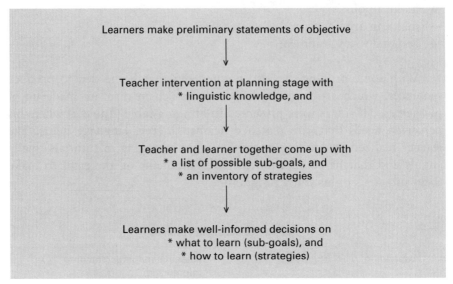

Figure 2   Model of Planning and Preparation Strategies

The advantages of teacher intervention at the planning and preparation stage of a self-instruction programme are obvious. Learners' initial statements of objective generally tend to be integrative and complex. It is important to make learners aware of the scope of their objectives so that they are clear about their commitment and responsibility in terms of time and energy.

Breaking the general objective into sub-goals also helps make the whole learning task more realistic and manageable, for example, in the selection of materials and management of time. In addition, the sub-goals established serve as a basis for criterial assessment of the learning programme. They help to remove much of the unease learners feel about checking their own progress.

When we make the job of managing their study and assessing their progress easier for learners, we are in fact inviting more learner participation and in turn enhancing motivation, which is the departure point on the road to learner autonomy.

ACKNOWLEDGEMENT

The quiz and general needs analysis used in the first stage of the project (see Appendices 1 and 2) were produced by the HKUST Self-Access Learner Training Team (Edward S.L. Li, Mabel C.P. Wong, Sarah Carmichael and Winnie W.F. Or).

APPENDIX 1

What's Self-Access Learning All About?

How much do you know about self-access learning? Here's a short quiz to test yourself before reading more about this approach to language learning.

Put True (T) or False (F) for the following statements.

No.	STATEMENTS	T/F
1.	You can choose to study materials that fit your interests and needs.	
2.	You have to come to the centre for a fixed period of time.	
3.	You should keep a record of the work you have done in the centre.	
4.	The work you have done will be corrected and your performance will be assessed by a teacher.	
5.	The teacher's presence is not necessary in the self-access centre.	
6.	You must always work on your own when you are doing self-access work.	
7.	You can use the computer to find the materials you want to use.	
8.	You can improve your pronunciation in the self-access centre.	
9.	Self-access learning must all be done in the self-access centre.	

Before checking your answers, you may want to look at some questions that people often ask about self-access learning. You may have asked similar questions before.

1. *Why self-access learning?*

Ans. Self-access learning refers to a way of learning language without the direct control of a teacher. There are different types of learners, with different language needs. Yours may not be the same as those of your friends. Moreover, your learning style and the pace you prefer to learn at may vary from those of others. It is logical and necessary that your individual needs and interests should be catered for.

2.   *What's wrong with classroom teaching?*

Ans. There is nothing wrong with it. Both classroom learning and self-access learning are valuable means to improve your language proficiency. They should be seen as complementary to each other. Whereas classroom learning follows a teacher-directed programme, self-access learning is based on a programme designed by yourself. You take full responsibility for your own learning in terms of analysing your needs, selecting materials, planning your work and assessing your own progress. By doing so, your learning would have a better chance of meeting your needs and interests.

3.   *Am I able to design my own learning programme?*

Ans. Definitely! Everyone can. Very often, you have opinions to offer to teachers on what you need in terms of material selection and teaching methods. Of course, you are not a professional language teacher. You may worry about your inability to analyse your own language deficiency. There are various back-up handouts which help you find out your language needs and plan your study.

4.   *Do I still need a teacher in self-access learning?*

Ans. In self-access learning, you take an active role in planning your learning. Your teacher is not in direct control of your learning. He/She, on the other hand, assumes a different role to facilitate learning in various ways, e.g. providing and organizing materials, giving advice when you need some, etc. You are not left alone in your own learning. Your teacher is always there for you to talk to and to support you. There is a teacher-consultant on duty in the centre whom you can approach for advice on any point in your study.

5.   *How different is a self-access centre from a language laboratory?*

Ans. In the self-access centre, materials are organized and catalogued in such a way as to facilitate individualized choice. A computer catalogue is available to help you search for materials under different language foci such as reading, grammar, pronunciation, etc. You can choose and access materials on your own. The materials are usually accompanied by answer keys and follow-up suggestions.

6. *How should I plan my study?*

Ans. You decide on what to learn according to your needs and interests. It is also your choice how long you want to spend in the self-access centre. Be realistic and take into account factors like urgency of your needs and availability of time. You will learn more effectively if you set aside a certain period of time and plan your goals. To help you do this, you can fill in a learner contract. It is also a good idea to keep a log book to record the materials you have used, your problems as well as your progress. You can plan what to do next. The log book will help you see what you have achieved and plan your next course of action to make your study systematic.

7. *Does self-access learning take place only in the self-access centre?*

Ans. There are many other ways of studying independently. The self-access centre contains a lot of useful materials and facilities. Other resources are also useful. You can use the library on campus where you can find a large collection of newspapers, magazines, journals as well as the main collection. In the AV area, there is a wide range of films, documentaries and TV programmes to choose. Even at home, you can find lots of opportunities to learn, such as watching English or Japanese TV programmes, listening to radio or reading newspapers, etc. Self-access learning can happen anywhere.

Do you feel that the answers have clarified some of your doubts? If you still have questions, feel free to talk to the consultant on duty.

Key	1. T 2. F 3. T 4. F 5. T 6. F 7. T 8. T 9. F

APPENDIX 2:   HKUST SELF-ACCESS CENTRE

General Needs Analysis

Welcome to the Self-Access Language Centre. Before you start any learning activities, we would like you to think about your own language needs and what you hope to achieve by visiting the centre. You should now complete the following sections.

Part 1: Needs Analysis

SECTION A: Personal information

Name: _____

Student No: _____

Year: _____

Department: _____

SECTION B: Assessing your present and future language needs

What do/will you need English for?
(e.g. academic communication, business communication, etc.)

Now	In the future

Who do/will you use English with?
(friends, tutors, inferiors, superiors, etc.)

Now	In the future

How often do/will you use English?

Now	In the future

SECTION C: What do you need most?

Below are some language foci you may need at present or in the future. Please tick the item(s) that you need most for improvement. You are not advised to choose all or too many because it would be more efficient if you could work consistently on a few areas at a time. In the last column, please put down a number (1 = very weak; 2 = rather weak; 3 = average; 4 = quite good; 5 = very good) to indicate your proficiency in each language focus you have ticked.

Language Focus	Needs		Proficiency
	Now	Future	
READING			
reading newspapers/magazines			
reading academic/professional articles			
reading documents			
leisure reading			
WRITING			
writing essays			
writing academic articles/papers			
writing curriculum vitae/resume			
writing instructions			
writing letters			
writing memos			
writing minutes			
writing reports			
LISTENING			
listening to documentaries			
listening to entertainments (e.g. movie)			
listening to interviews			
listening to lectures and notetaking			
listening to TV/radio news			
listening to business meetings			
listening to telephone conversations			
SPEAKING			
holding social conversations			
taking part in group discussions			
having interviews			
giving presentations			
holding telephone conversations			
GRAMMAR			
PRONUNCIATION			
VOCABULARY			
others			

If you want to have a thorough analysis of these language foci, read the individual handouts on how to select relevant materials. They will help you analyze your own problems and needs in greater detail. They will also give you advice on selection of materials in the centre to suit your needs.

From the above table, you may have already identified a few language foci that you want to work on. Usually they are those you regard as very important (either for your present or future life) but difficult.

Now pick the most important one and break it down into smaller sub-goals (e.g. sub-goals for 'reading academic articles' could be 'locating main ideas', 'identifying major and minor details', 'summarizing and note-taking' and so on). Knowing what sub-goals you have will help you break down your target into some manageable units. This will also help you allocate your time more sensibly when you formulate your own learning schedule.

Target language focus:

_____

Sub-goals:

1. _____

2. _____

3. _____

4. _____

5. _____

SECTION D: Planning your learning

Now you may have already found out what areas of English you need to improve. Before you design a study plan which helps you achieve your personal objectives, you need to think about your own learning style. Answer the following questions.

How much time will you be able to spend in the Self-Access Language Laboratory per week?

_____

Which learning style do you prefer?
____ work on your own, on materials that you have selected
____ work on your own, with regular guidance from the Self-Access Language Centre consultant
____ work with other students as a small group

What are your strengths and weaknesses in using English?
(e.g. personality traits or studying habits which make learning easier or more difficult for you)

Strengths	Weaknesses

How can you make the full use of your strengths and overcome your weaknesses?

_____

_____

_____

Part 2: Learner Contract

It's time for you to decide how you are going to commit your time and effort to your learning. Consider the information you have given in Section D carefully and try to set a realistic goal for yourself. (You should set only one goal for each contract.) Fill out the contract and discuss it with a consultant.

****

Period of time this plan covers (Day/Month):

_____

Goal: By the end of this period, I should be able to

_____

How are you going to learn what you have noted above?

_____

_____

How are you going to assess your achievement?

_____

I am going to meet the consultant _____ times a week/a month to talk about my progress.

Date & Time	Sub-Goal(s)	Number of hours	Activities	Materials	Remarks

Signed _____   Consultant _____

Date _____

CHAPTER 6

What Is the Fare to the Land of Effective Language Learning?

Beatrice Ma , English Language Teaching Unit, The Chinese University of Hong Kong

INTRODUCTION

FARE is a seven-day programme that trains learners to utilize, for self-directed language learning, the resources of the Independent Learning Centre (ILC) at the Chinese University of Hong Kong (CUHK). The name has two levels of meaning. It can be seen as the means used to reach a certain destination or a stage of accomplishment (like a bus fare), and, it is also an acronym for Flexible learning approaches, Accessible resources, Responsible learners and Enjoyable learning experience.

The first three days of the programme is an orientation component which deconditions learners from their past language learning experience and provides them with a new perspective on language learning. The other four days introduce common language situations and offer suggestions for tackling them. After the programme learners can pursue a self-directed Language Improvement Plan. An outline of the programme can be seen in Figure 1.

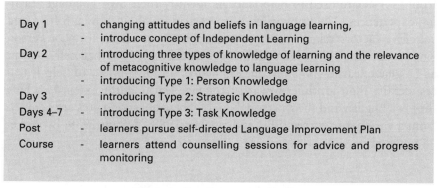

Day 1	-	changing attitudes and beliefs in language learning,
	-	introduce concept of Independent Learning
Day 2	-	introducing three types of knowledge of learning and the relevance of metacognitive knowledge to language learning
	-	introducing Type 1: Person Knowledge
Day 3	-	introducing Type 2: Strategic Knowledge
Days 4–7	-	introducing Type 3: Task Knowledge
Post	-	learners pursue self-directed Language Improvement Plan
Course	-	learners attend counselling sessions for advice and progress monitoring

Figure 1 Fare Programme Outline

DAY ONE OF THE PROGRAMME

There are four activities on the first day.
1. 'I'll tell you what it is' is a lego rebuilding game. It is designed to make learners aware of the strategies they use in tackling a task of a vague and uninformed nature.
2. 'Help' addresses the problems of peer dominance in a self-directed learning situation. If individuals dominate in class a teacher can interfere, self-directed learners need to learn to resolve such problems themselves.
3. 'No sweat, no gain' stresses the importance of learner responsibility in effective language learning. Learners are given a passage adapted from Holec (1987) on learner responsibility and are asked to comment on his views and propose ways to carry out his suggestions.
4. 'The moral of these games' concludes the preliminary activities and introduces the concept of independent learning. This is intended to overcome teacher dependence.

DAY TWO OF THE PROGRAMME

From this point onwards metacognitive knowledge plays an important part in the programme. For language learners, metacognitive knowledge includes beliefs, insights and concepts that they have acquired about language and the language learning process. This programme follows Falvell's (1979) three-type classification of Person Knowledge, Strategic Knowledge and Task Knowledge.

Person Knowledge is introduced on day two. This is the general knowledge that learners have about the 'laws of human learning' and is thus a useful tool with which learners can equip themselves. Person Knowledge includes what learners know about themselves as learners. Two case-studies from CUHK are used to help learners identify their own language learning experiences. The knowledge learners acquire about how affective and cognitive factors relate to their own experience is also a form of Person Knowledge. Such knowledge influences the formation of their self-concept as language learners. Survey questionnaires are distributed to help learners identify their attitudes towards language learning, the extent to which they use English and their personal goals. These questionnaires are adapted from a variety of sources (Ellis and Sinclair 1989; Willing 1989; Broder et al. undated).

DAY THREE OF THE PROGRAMME

This day introduces Strategic Knowledge of language learning which can be defined as knowledge of 'effective strategies' and 'principles of learning'. 'Strategies' is a vague concept for our learners so the day begins with a short quiz to help them identify the nature of strategies. After that, learners are offered some definitions of effective strategies. Language tasks are then distributed to each group of learners to formulate a strategy or a set of strategies for solving language problems.

In the second part of Day 3 the 'Principles of Learning' are introduced and self-management is emphasized. Learners are encouraged to use a planning guide. The plan includes signing a contract and keeping a practice activity log for self-monitoring and counsellor reference.

DAYS FOUR TO SEVEN OF THE PROGRAMME

The second half of the programme deals with the concept of Task Knowledge. This is done through two strategy workshops, one on listening and the other on building vocabulary through reading. There are four listening tasks; listening for gist, listening for details, prediction and guessing, and finally utilizing other means for listening. Learners are shown how to tackle these tasks which prepares them for independent language learning.

THE LANGUAGE IMPROVEMENT PLAN

After the induction programme, the learners optionally agree a plan of practice activities which they then undertake independently. An activity log is supplied to record the nature, situation and assessment of the contracted practice activity. Learners are also asked to keep a record of their own comments on the situation and mood when the practice activity takes place.

EVALUATION

Forty-five students have participated in the FARE programme, of these eighteen also opted to follow the Language Improvement Plan. From their records, it is obvious that the learners are not making full use of their logs. These logs are intended to facilitate counselling without which counsellors have to retrieve information directly from the learners. The process, though lengthy, has proved to be useful because it helps learners focus on their problems and identify strategies more quickly.

After completing the plan learners can exit from the programme or continue to use other practice activities. Half of the eighteen participants in the plan have started the next stage of their language improvement plan voluntarily or on counsellor's advice.

Ninety percent of students evaluating the programme have been positive and encouraging. They felt the approach was new, interesting and helpful. Materials were generally considered appropriate, interesting and helpful. All respondents requested more practice on the suggested practice activities.

CONCLUSION

Training learners to use strategies in learning English is not new. The FARE programme is a more organized effort in bringing the learners to an awareness of their own learning characteristics and a knowledge of English. Learner training programmes can not replace normal classroom instruction. The evaluation feedback and observation from counselling sessions have shown that only those learners who are conscious of their needs and objectives can benefit from such an approach.

The encouraging and constructive feedback from the participants shows that learner training is necessary, especially in a tertiary setting where students should be open to more choices and given more flexibility in choosing a suitable learning mode. Learners should be encouraged to keep a learning log in which they can fully utilize their own Strategic Knowledge in language learning. The present system still requires development. Counselling in a self-directed learning situation is important in helping learners learn. It is also a rich area in second language acquisition research.

REFERENCES

Broder, C., Brown, K., Forester, B. and Kaufmann, R. (undated) 'Parispanny Adult and Community Education Centre, workshop materials'. Cited in A. Wenden, 1991. *Learner Strategies For Learner Autonomy*. Prentice Hall International.

Ellis, G. and Sinclair, B., 1989. *Learning to Learn English*. Cambridge: Cambridge University Press.

Falvell, J. 1979. 'Metacognition and cognitive monitoring: a new area of cognitive developmental inquiry'. *American Psychologist* 34:906–11.

Holec, H. 1987. 'The learner as manager: managing learning or managing to learn' in A. Wenden and J. Rubin (eds.) *Learner Strategies in Language Learning*. London: Prentice Hall.

Willing, K. 1989. *Teaching How to Learn*. National Centre for English Language Teaching and Research: Macquarie University, Sydney, Australia.

Self-Access Logs: Promoting Self-Directed Learning

Elaine Martyn, English Centre, The University of Hong Kong

INTRODUCTION

> If [an educator] is indeed wise he does not bid you enter the house
> of his wisdom but rather leads you to the threshold of your own
> mind (quoted in Tompkins and McGraw 1988:172).

Kahlil Gibran wrote these words in 1923, but they remain an item of
faith, if not action, for many educators today. This drive to encourage
autonomous, independent, or self-directed learning is one of the key forces
behind the development of self-access centres for language learning.

As has been noted by Sheerin (1989), a self-access centre (SAC) full of
fine resources and advanced equipment does not necessarily lead to this
desired type of learning. In fact, programmed self-access learning materials may lead to greater dependence than many of today's classrooms;
however in such an environment, a student is likely to feel safe enough to
venture alone. In contrast, some independent students may simply get lost
in the gold mine of resources. This dichotomy may raise questions for
teachers who favour the ideological rationale 'that self-access or autonomous learning is a valuable goal, increasing motivation, independence,
and therefore, enthusiasm to learn' (Miller and Rogerson-Revell 1993:230)
and who also believe that self-access is a pedagogical approach beneficial
to the development of language learning skills.

This paper describes an on-going study of how to 'guide' students
without being prescriptive or losing them in a maze of resources. The
guiding mechanism used is a self-access log, a tool for negotiations between teachers and learners. It is similar to the learning contract of Knowles
(1975), but is expanded to include a record of work and reflection on
learning. The contract or learning agreement, and thus the negotiations
between teacher and learner, is based on a concept of decision-making
where one of the clear assumptions is that students must have goals, that

is, they must know why they are doing what they are doing. While this need not be the first decision made, nor need it be the learner's or teacher's prime factor; it is clearly headlined in the log.

Two concerns which are often raised in regards to a self-directed learning model in an institutional setting will be addressed briefly. Firstly, it is true that not all learners want to be self-directed nor are they all capable of the degree of independence necessary for autonomous learning. However, such learners cannot make a free choice between self- or teacher-directed learning until they are capable of carrying out both (Holec 1987:147). Only when students have developed learning management skills, have they a real choice. The log and supporting negotiations are designed so that the teacher may adapt the level of control and support given according to the degree of independence of the learner (and their own level of comfort, a point highlighted by Nakhoul [1993]), and thus build learning management skills gradually. In addition, for the learners in this study, self-access was just one component of their course of study, in which one-third of class time was designated for self-access and tutorial work.

Secondly, while writers such as Brookfield (1985) might see a learning contract as too restrictive, it should be recognized that designing and negotiating a learning contract is not the end of the process but the starting point. If in the process of fulfilling a contract a learner finds a new and worth while direction, any contract is renegotiable. In fact, it is important to help learners to do this, not only for self-access work but for improving language learning in general. Dickinson also points to the value of teachers helping learners to 'understand that decisions on objectives can be dynamic; that is, they can change in response to a developing understanding of one's wants and needs and of one's own language learning' (1992:9).

After a review of key terms as they are interpreted in this paper and a description of the overall design of the study, the three-phased evolution of the log will be presented through a discussion of rationale and objectives, the log itself and the outcomes.

KEY TERMS

While the following terms will be familiar to most readers, it is important to define the sense in which they are used in this paper.

Self-Access Learning

Self-access learning refers to students' direct access to language learning resources, but it also entails some degree of learner decision-making, such as choices in: time, place, pacing, materials, learning strategies, objectives, methods, monitoring and assessment. Self-access thus allows teachers and students to shift the responsibility for learning along the continuum from teacher or materials-directed to self-directed or even autonomous learning. This shift can occur by increasing the number of decisions taken by the learner when both the teacher and the student are ready. Resources for self-access language learning are likely to be most available in a SAC, but learners need not limit themselves to these resources.

Self-Directed Learning Skills

Self-directed or learner-managed learning skills are the skills required to plan, carry out and assess an appropriate learning programme, in this case in language learning. In this study the skills emphasized are negotiation and decision-making, and the ability and commitment to carry out the learning programme with the support of a teacher in the role of counsellor, helper, consultant, facilitator, etc.

Self-Access Logs

The self-access log described here is a secondary though guiding tool for negotiations and relations between teachers and learners. It functions as a learning contract, a record of work, a place for reflection and a guide for negotiations between teachers and learners. It focuses on the decision-making process in learning and encourages student-managed learning. Its three essential components are a plan, records of work and self-assessment.

Learning Negotiations

Learning negotiations refer to the process of shared decision-making between teachers and learners about language learning. Negotiations are not only a precursor to language study and learning, but an integral part of the process which allows for a shift in focus as learners refine their objectives or perhaps embrace new challenges from those originally perceived as relevant. This approach follows that of Tompkins and McGraw who believe that the focus of what they term contracting 'should be on the process: the relationship between student and teacher and the negotiation that occurs throughout the learning experience' (1988:173).

THE DESIGN

The learners mentioned in this study are first year arts students at the University of Hong Kong, an English medium university, who are taking a required but non-credit earning English course. Most are about eighteen years old and have already studied English for a number of years.

This paper traces the development of the self-access log in three phases over a period of three academic years. In Phase 1, the logs of twelve students in one of the writer's classes were reviewed. Phase 1 took place during the second semester of the first year of the study, the year in which self-access was introduced as a course component. It served as a preliminary test of the application of self-directed learning principles to self-access learning through the use of the self-access log. Phase 2 took place during the second year of the study. As a large scale trial, it involved a review of the logs of 107 students out of a total of 542 students registered in the English for Arts course that year (approximately 20%). The selection of logs was dependent on teachers voluntarily passing them on to the researcher for a short period of time. Phase 3, the current and final phase, is once again small-scale including the logs of only fifteen students, it focuses on refinement of the log and in-depth study of how it has been used by these students.

PHASE 1

Rationale and Objectives

Before beginning this study it became obvious that simply encouraging students to work in the SAC, with fairly informal reporting back to a tutorial group had little effect, i.e. it promoted little self-access study. When students were asked to write a short activity plan, the level of involvement increased appreciably. However, this 'supermarket' approach (Miller and Rogerson-Revell 1993) seemed rather superficial, placing too much emphasis simply on the activity, e.g. watching a video, rather than on the purpose, e.g. improving listening comprehension of American English.

The action research objective of Phase 1, therefore, was to facilitate students' self-access study so that they would become managers of their own learning process through: (1) setting objectives, (2) designing a learning programme, (3) monitoring their learning and (4) self-assessing the outcome. The work in the self-access log was supported by pair work and by pair tutorials, which involved negotiations, support and assessment.

The Log

In Phase 1 pairs of students kept a joint log. On the planning page, there were three questions which were discussed and the responses clarified in tutorial negotiations:
1. What is your joint learning objective for this semester?
2. What plans do you have to meet this objective?
3. How do you plan to assess whether you have met your objective?

Each record of a self-access session included four points:
1. What did you do? (brief step-by-step summary)
2. Quick reactions.
3. Do you think this session has helped you work towards your learning objective? Why/why not?
4. Plan for the next self-access session.

The self-assessment focused on learning objectives, methods of assessment and progress in language learning as well as pair work.

During the three tutorials held during the semester, an attempt was made to develop an open and egalitarian climate, the learners were encouraged and information was collected on the learners' progress. Also in the tutorials both students and teacher gave ratings for task completion, level of motivation and awareness of learning.

Outcomes

Logs were not always kept up-to-date, but all students had completed them satisfactorily by the end of the semester. As a planning device, the log encouraged careful thought; however, the session-by-session advance planning section of the record page was usually left blank. The log served the teacher as a useful monitor and was also a good starting point for tutorial discussions. Through the use of the log and negotiations, students clarified their objectives, methods of learning and ideas on assessment.

Half of the students reported that before using the logs they either had no objectives or did not remember them. In contrast, with the log, goals became a major focal point. During Phase 1, nine out of twelve students selected a combination of listening and speaking objectives within specified contexts, e.g. daily conversations, academic study or American films. Two focused only on listening and one on reading. During this phase about a third of the students refined or shifted their objectives closer in line with their needs and the resources available. Overall, students' awareness of learning objectives increased, their expression of objectives, though general (in linguistic terms), became clearer, and they were able to select appropriate learning activities.

Eleven of the students' learning activities involved watching videos or listening to lectures and participating in discussions, most often related to the listening/viewing they had completed. A few students also participated in other conversations and discussions. Responses to the question, 'What did you do?' on the record pages were very brief, such as a few steps, resources used or content summaries. Notations in a few logs indicated how they changed their approach during the semester. Although students were able to select and carry out activities appropriate to their goals, only a few were able to focus their goals specifically or record much refinement of their process of learning.

Pair work proved to be very motivating for half the students, but problematic for the others. Building friendships was an important outcome for some, and one which encouraged them to do their self-access work. However, most identified planning the time for sessions as difficult. For unsuccessful pairs, it was important to allow regrouping and individual study. Pair self-access was therefore a good innovation, but one which should not have been applied so broadly. Its success appeared to be primarily dependent on pair compatibility (in terms of time, interest and personality).

Regular self-assessment and monitoring kept the learners' attention focused on their learning process and progress. Students gave a quick reaction and comments on whether each session had helped them work towards their learning objective in their logs. Comments in the quick reaction section, included level of difficulty in use of English, feelings towards videos or discussions and information or knowledge gained. Responses ranged from personal or emotional to analytic. Almost all appeared useful, either in assessing SAC materials and/or contributing to the student/teacher negotiations.

Students' measures of learning were mostly qualitative, e.g. judgements based on partners' agreement on the meaning of videos, level of participation in a discussion group or estimates of the percentage of time spent speaking Cantonese versus English. Quantitative estimates and counts were made by some, e.g. number of pages read in an hour, number of errors on worksheets, or number of new words learned. With hindsight, perhaps more precise quantitative measures would have been useful, but the 'measures' used helped students monitor their progress easily.

Students reported 78% of their self-access sessions had helped them work towards their learning objective. Comments on the remaining 22% of sessions were split equally between responses that were unclear or negative. Reasons given for negative answers included: too much use of Chinese (in video or conversation), English level was too easy and lack of opportunity to speak.

Retrospective ratings were made of task completion, motivation and awareness of learning prior to Phase 1. Students continued to rate themselves at each tutorial during the phase. Prior to using the logs, 50% of the students reported successful completion of their self-access work, ie. they gave themselves a rating of 3 or 4 on a 5 point scale. The success rate increased dramatically in this category after the log was used in Phase 1 of this study: all students gave themselves a rating of 3 or 4 (moderately complete or higher). The teacher/researcher's rating was in complete agreement on this point. In terms of motivation, the ratings indicated either maintenance or increase in motivation, ie. their ratings either remained at 3 or moved up to 4 when the log was used. Interestingly the teacher/ researcher made generally higher ratings based on the level of interest and even enthusiasm expressed at tutorials as well as on the increased times spent doing self-access work. In contrast, students rated their awareness of learning more highly (at 3 or 4) than the teacher/researcher who assigned ratings of 2 or 3. Nevertheless, the ratings indicated a general increase in task completion, motivation and awareness of learning based on subjective ratings of both learners and teacher.

The time spent on self-access study also increased after the log was introduced. The minimum expectation for self-access study was one hour per week or a total of ten hours during Phase 1. The mean time spent by each student averaged 12 hours with a range from 8 to 18 hours (number of sessions: 5 to 10, length of sessions: 0.5 to 3 hours). An interesting correspondence between stable, compatible pairs and a greater amount of time spent on self-access study was observed.

PHASE 2

The log was revised for Phase 2 and its use expanded: it was recommended for all students taking the English for Arts course. Logs were submitted to the researcher by eleven teachers from fifteen classes. The results of the analysis of 107 students' self-access logs are reported below.

Rationale and Objectives

The Phase 2 log was designed to integrate the complete self-directed learning cycle into the actual log, (from needs analysis through to self-assessment) and also to ease teacher monitoring of self-access study, the importance of which had been highlighted in an earlier study (Martyn and Chan 1992). Teacher monitoring was identified as important for two reasons; firstly, it appeared to encourage more commitment on the part of students and secondly, it tended to increase teachers' security in a self-access approach to language learning. Thus the log became much more explicit and detailed than the one used in Phase 1.

The prime objectives for the Phase 2 log were to develop self-directed learning skills and to act as a catalyst for teacher/student learning negotiations. It was important to discover whether the materials and approach of the Phase 1 log could be extended to a range of teachers with a broad spectrum of views on self-access learning.

The Log

The Phase 2 log had ten sections:
1. schedule of (teacher/student) meetings,
2. exploring needs and wants,
3. setting goals,
4. planning your learning programme,
5. study plan,
6. teacher's comments,
7. record of work,
8. teacher's comments,
9. assessment/evaluation,
10. ideas for self-assessment (information only).

Details related to goals, record of work and assessment/evaluation were included in the log to clarify its logic.

Before setting goals, students were asked to explore their *own* needs and wants, by writing three completions to the following statement: 'I think I'll have difficulty with my studies if I don't learn to do these things better:' and then to note when and how they had discovered these needs. They were also asked for three things they 'would like to do better for personal reasons'.

There were then three pages on setting goals, planning a learning programme and study plan (Table 1) which were intended to guide the flow of thinking and negotiations from goal to action. Students were encouraged to focus on two or three skills which they wished to improve.

Six record-of-work pages were included (one per session), which required logistical details: date, time, materials, etc.; a brief step-by-step summary of what was done; a quick reaction and self-assessment.

The self/log assessment at the end of the log asked students to rate and comment on their learning and the log as a learning tool. First they rated how effectively they had met their goals on a five point scale, from 'met almost none of my goals' (1) to 'met nearly all of my goals' (5). Next

Table 1   Planning a Learning Programme: From Goals to Action

Setting Goals	Planning Your Learning Programme	Study Plan
Goal No. . . . (I want to be better able to . . .)	What can I do to achieve this goal? Where can I find what I need? Who can help me? How can I check my performance on each activity?	Goal No. . . . To be completed by (day/month) Ways to achieve it

they rated how much the log had helped them, from 'very little' (1) to 'very much' (5). Finally, they were asked for short written comments.

Results

107 Phase 2 logs were analysed in detail in terms of goals, records of work and self-assessment.

Three goals were recorded in 80% of the logs, which equalled the number of spaces available. As indicated by Table 2 listening and speaking goals were the most popular: the factors influencing selection of goals is a matter of speculation but may include: needs, interests, resources available in the SAC or teachers' advice. However, it is clear that the follow-through, with generally appropriate activities, varied considerably between skills. Receptive skills, for which there are more self-access and library resources ranked highest in terms of follow-up. Ninety-four percent of the listening objectives were followed by records of listening sessions,[1] for reading the figure was 70%, for speaking 55% and for writing 39%. The reasons for these differences are unclear: it could be that the productive skills are covered sufficiently in the classroom or that the SAC lacks appropriate resources in these areas. Parallel to this, it can be seen from Table 2 that the goals added by students were also predominantly in the receptive skills areas.

Table 2   Goals Selected and Follow-through

Goals	Initially Selected	Goals acted upon	No Sessions	Goals Added
Listening	82	77	5	14
Speaking	75	41	34	2
Reading	48	34	14	10
Writing	46	18	28	2
Other *	52			

* Includes vocabulary, grammar, learning word-processing. No further analysis of this figure is given.

Table 3 shows a broad range in the number of sessions recorded in the log (from 2–16). 62% of the logs indicated 5–8 sessions, but 31% only recorded 2–4. The average length of session was 67 minutes (based on 89 individual logs in which records of time were complete). The average total amount of self-access study recorded was just over 5 hours (354 minutes) per log. This is clearly less than the average time noted in Phase 1 of this project.

Table 3   Records of Work

No. of Sessions Recorded	No. of Logs
2–4	33
5–8	67
9–12	6
13–16	1
Total	107

The self/log assessment was completed in 50 individual logs, Table 4 summarizes the results. Half of the students (52%) rated themselves at the mid-point in terms of meeting their goals, with 32% more positive. The ratings on the log offer a clear indication of its comparable degree of usefulness (Table 5). It was seen as most helpful in setting goals (54% positive) and least helpful in planning (38% – negative), with monitoring progress neutral (48% – neutral).

Table 4   Self-assessment of Meeting Learning Goals

Rating Scale	1	2	3	4	5
Responses	0	8	26	15	1
Proportion	16%		52%	32%	

Key: 1 = Met almost none of my goals.   5 = Met nearly all of my goals.

Table 5   Student Assessment of Usefulness of the Log

Rating Scale	1	2	3	4	5
The log helped me set realistic goals.	0	9 (18%)	14 (28%)	24 (54%)	3
The log helped me plan appropriate learning activities.	0	9 (38%)	15 (30%)	13 (32%)	3
The log helped me keep track of progress.	1	8 (18%)	24 (48%)	15 (34%)	2

Key: 1 = Very little.   5 = Very much.

In addition to the results from these assessments we should consider comments from three of the teachers who participated in Phase 2 of the study. On the positive side two teachers described the log as 'making their job easier' and 'extremely useful because it provides a focus for dialogue'. All three also confirmed the findings of a survey of teachers' attitudes (Martyn and Voller 1993), in which the following comments were noted: 'a lot of built-in guidance' and 'useful . . . it focuses students on tasks and provides opportunities for practical feedback.' The basic weakness of the Phase 2 log was best summarized by one teacher who wrote, 'too long, too unclear, repetitive' (Martyn and Voller 1993:105).

PHASE 3

Rationale and Objectives

The objectives for the current phase of this project are to follow up on log usage within one class where the self-directed learning approach is stressed.

The Log

The Phase 3 log is intended to be more self-accessible than earlier versions. In both the log itself and teacher support materials, there is an emphasis on building student learning skills and shifting responsibility for learning to students.

Similar to Log 2, the Phase 3 log focuses on individual students' learning preferences, needs and concerns regarding language learning. However, this time it is done only through brain-storming and discussion. In both student and teacher materials the log focuses on five decisions (with encouragement to shift the decision-making power from teacher to learner over the academic year):
1. What is your learning objective?
2. What materials and strategies will you use?
3. How long will you spend on this learning project?
4. How will you show you have accomplished your objective?
5. How and by whom will your learning be evaluated?

The first two contracts in the Phase 3 log offer guided decision-making in practical areas which are intended to prepare students for more independent decision-making. Contract 1 is an orientation to the SAC; contract 2 is an exploratory contract focusing on a language skill area. Built-in guidance includes suggestions or answers to some of the above five questions.

The third contract is more self-directed with students (individually or in pairs) selecting to do self-access study on more specific areas, usually following up on a skill area which the student will have explored in the second contract.

CONCLUSION

This study has identified three factors which influence the success of self-access language learning in general and self-directed learning specifically:

1. Document design features are critical as they shape both type and level of response, e.g. the Phase 2 log was too complex and cognitively demanding thus demotivating for many students (and teachers).

2. Social and co-operative aspects of learning have often been given short shrift in the emphasis on individualization and independence in self-access learning. This study points to the value of these: group and teacher support are essential to developing self-directed and autonomous learning skills, as illustrated in Phase 1 and developing in Phase 3.

3. The importance of teacher autonomy has also become more evident. While teacher autonomy was not intended to be an item for study, the teacher's influence became evident in reviewing class sets of logs in Phase 2, e.g. in terms of degree of completion and linkage between goals and records of work. The self-access log is not the best way for all teachers to develop self-access skills; it only works if it matches the teacher's pedagogical or philosophical framework.

Finally, this study has shown that a self-access log can be used as a tool to heighten students' awareness of language and learning. This is a worthwhile outcome, considering the value placed on cognitive and metacognitive awareness in recent research. However, while students have proven themselves able to work through the cycle of self-directed learning and set general communicative goals within a specified context, they have not set specific linguistic ones, which Dickinson (1992:4) has emphasized as important. Perhaps this will again prove to be a teacher-dependent factor.

Thus the self-access log appears to be an effective tool for the promotion of self-directed learning; however, it must be recognized that it is only a tool. Its success will be dependent on the quality of the teacher/learner relationship and negotiations which it is intended to foster.

NOTE

1. This figure is actually confused by the inclusion of some assigned self-access videos (regardless of students' stated self-access goals) and also assigned course related self-access work which generally involved watching videos in the SAC.

REFERENCES

Brookfield, S. 1985. 'Self-directed learning: a critical review of research', in S. Brookfield (ed.) *Self-directed Learning: From Theory to Practice* (New Directions for Continuing Education, No. 25). San Francisco: Jossey-Bass.

Dickinson, L. 1992. *Learner Autonomy 2: Learner Training for Language Learning.* Dublin: Authentik.

Holec, H. 1987. 'The learner as manager: managing learning or managing to learn', in A. Wenden and J. Rubens (eds.) *Learner Strategies and Language Learning.* Englewood Cliffs, NJ: Prentice Hall.

Knowles, M. 1975. *Self-Directed Learning: A Guide for Learners and Teachers.* New York, Cambridge: The Adult Education Company.

Martyn, E. and Chan, N.Y. 1992. 'Self-access action research: a progress report'. *Hongkong Papers in Linguistics and Language Teaching* 15:59–68.

Martyn, E. and Voller, P. 1993. 'Teachers' attitudes to self-access learning'. *Hongkong Papers in Linguistics and Language Teaching* 16:103–10.

Miller, L. and Rogerson-Revell, P. 1993. 'Self-access systems'. *ELT Journal* 47(3):228–33.

Nakhoul, E. 1993. 'Letting go', in J. Edge and K. Richards (eds.), *Teachers Develop Teachers Research: Papers on Classroom Research and Teacher Development.* Oxford: Heinemann.

Sheerin, S. 1989. *Self-access.* Oxford: Oxford University Press.

Tompkins, C. and McGraw, M.J. (1988). 'The negotiated learning contract', in D. Boud (ed.) *Developing Student Autonomy in Learning.* London: Kogan-Page.

CHAPTER 8

Training Learners for Independence

Deirdre Moynihan Tong, English Language Study-Centre,
Hong Kong Polytechnic

INTRODUCTION

This paper describes the Speaking Skills module of a learner training programme in use at the Hong Kong Polytechnic English Language Study-Centre. It also discusses in detail the piloting of that module, its evaluation and implications for future development.

BACKGROUND

During term time, the English Language Study-Centre is open only to students who attend a service-English course and have been identified by their service-English teachers as requiring supplementary tuition (in practice, the weakest 20% of a class). These students are referred to the Study-Centre for a compulsory twenty-hour programme. They attend in groups of between two and five and are provided with 100% teacher contact time.

In summer, the centre is open to all Polytechnic students. The Summer Programme is voluntary and students usually attend in groups which are expected to share a teacher. They receive between 30% and 50% teacher contact time. The popularity of the Summer Programme has lead to the decision that in the near future the benefits of the Study-Centre will be extended, during term-time, to all students who wish to attend on a voluntary basis. Such students will be encouraged to attend in groups and will be expected to study independently, although a counsellor will be available to provide help and advice.

A learner training programme is particularly appropriate for the Summer Programme students and for the future term-time voluntary students, as they are required to work independently for part of the time. In addition, as voluntary students, they are generally highly motivated but do need some help to benefit fully from the programme.

RATIONALE

In their first visit all Summer Programme students are introduced to the Centre and to the aims of the programme, which are to: improve language skills, improve confidence, and promote learner independence.

It is explained that, in becoming more independent, the students will be better able to attend to their language needs, both now and in the future.

In the second session learners perform a needs analysis which is then used to draw up a programme of study with a teacher. This approach allows the students to make their own choices, but with the guidance of a teacher where necessary. The students vary in their response to this opportunity: some accept it immediately, some are initially hesitant but soon see the advantages of making their own choices, while others experience difficulty as they are unaccustomed to making these types of choices.

Although one of the aims of the summer programme is to help the learners to become more independent, insufficient initial training was being provided to enable learners to achieve this aim. A learner training programme would raise awareness of different language learning strategies and provide an opportunity to practise these strategies. It would also help learners to identify their own learning styles and build up confidence in their ability to learn independently.

PROGRAMME DESIGN FEATURES

A Modular Approach

A survey (undertaken in summer 1993) suggests that students' primary interest is in the area of speaking skills (see Lai and Mak 1992). However, a substantial number are interested in other skills and other areas such as grammar and vocabulary. A modular approach, with each module focusing on an individual skill or other aspect such as grammar or vocabulary, should meet this requirement. This will allow students to focus on 'learning how to learn' in the areas of language they are particularly interested in. It will also allow the programme to be integrated with the language programme drawn up following the needs analysis.

Selecting A Learner Strategies Classification

A number of different systems have been devised for classifying learning strategies (Oxford 1990; O'Malley and Chamot 1990). Oxford divides

strategies into direct strategies and indirect strategies. The former are defined as those which 'directly involve the target language' (1990:37) and consist of:
- memory strategies: those that help learners remember,
- cognitive strategies: those that involve manipulating or transforming the target structure,
- compensation strategies: those that enable learners to use new language despite gaps in their knowledge; for example, paraphrasing.

Indirect Strategies are defined as those which 'support and manage the language learning process without (in many instances) directly involving the target language' (Oxford 1990:135). These consist of:
- metacognitive strategies: those that relate to managing the learning process,
- affective strategies: those that are concerned with how the learner feels about language learning,
- social strategies: those that involve interacting with others.

O'Malley and Chamot (1990) have a three-way classification, which incorporates the same elements as that of Oxford (1990). Their strategies are:
- cognitive (they subsume memory strategies under this heading),
- metacognitive,
- social and affective.

Rubin (1981, cited in O'Malley and Chamot 1990) also classifies strategies into those that directly affect learning and those that indirectly affect learning. However, her classification is less comprehensive than Oxford's. In addition, she sees compensation strategies as contributing indirectly to learning rather than directly.

Although the classification systems vary, the writers identify may of the same individual strategies. Oxford's classification was chosen since it incorporates a user test, the Strategy Inventory for Language Learning (SILL), that enables learners to judge their strategy use, and a teacher's guide.

Reasons for Designing Materials In-House

Initially, 'Learning to Learn English' (Ellis and Sinclair 1989) was considered as a basis for our materials but was rejected for three reasons:
1. Some of the examples might be perceived as irrelevant by our learners. For example, the vocabulary exercise on page 38 relies on a

knowledge of London landmarks that we felt the learners might not possess.

2. Many students might want to focus on only one or two modules and would, therefore, be unwilling to purchase the textbook without which they would have nothing to refer back to.

3. Materials specifically designed for our students would be more effective than a textbook aimed at a wider audience. Furthermore, this approach meant that practice materials from a wide range of ELT course books could be combined into a single package.

Materials from a Range of ELT Sources

Although the programme as a whole is specifically designed for learners at Hong Kong Polytechnic, the practice activities are taken from a wide range of commercially available materials. There are two reasons for this: firstly, it gives the programme more variety and, secondly, it helps the learners become familiar with a wide range of materials. This is important as, in order to learn independently, learners need to be able to assess the suitability of learning materials.

SPEAKING SKILLS MODULE DESIGN

A Popular Skill

Speaking is the focus for the first learner training module since it is the skill most frequently requested at the Study-Centre but the one which learners get few opportunities to practise. In addition, some learners have difficulty practising because they feel they need to speak to a teacher or a native speaker. Another problem is that learners may feel ill at ease practising their English outside a context associated with speaking English. One of the pilot groups explained that they would feel uncomfortable speaking English to each other in public as people would think that they were showing off. The Study-Centre provides a place where it is acceptable to speak English.

The Strategies Questionnaire

A strategies questionnaire was devised for the module (other modules will also have individualized strategies questionnaires). The questionnaire is modelled on Oxford's SILL test (1990) but is shorter as it only contains examples of strategies appropriate for the particular skill or area of focus in the module.

The purpose of the Strategies Questionnaire is two-fold. Firstly, it serves as a measure of how the learners perceive their own strategy use at the beginning of the course, and can be used again later to measure any change in their use of strategies. Secondly, it previews the rest of the module and starts a discussion of strategy use enabling the teacher to gauge how familiar the students are with different strategies.

Programme Design

It is very important that as much practice as possible is given to strategy use, since students might react negatively if they feel they are not getting the opportunity to practise and improve their English, that is, spending too much time 'learning to learn' and not enough time 'learning the language'. Furthermore, it is important that students see how they can use the strategies and experience for themselves how effective these are. This allows them to see which strategies they enjoy and find useful and those that do not appeal to them.

Programme Elements

The programme consists of ten sections which are detailed below:
1. Introduction and Strategies Questionnaire
    These aim to explore the students' feelings about English, introduce the idea of strategies and look at their current use of some strategies related to speaking. Quotes from other students are used to provide a basis for discussion (in the pilot, quotes were from Ellis and Sinclair [1989]).
2. Pronunciation
    This section introduces different aspects of pronunciation (sounds, word stress, sentence stress, features of connected speech and intonation) and familiarizes students with the pronunciation materials available in the Study-Centre.
3. The Differences between Spoken and Written English
    This aims to examine the differences between written and spoken English.
4. Social Strategies
    This section contains a variety of social strategies, for example, asking questions and seeking clarification.
5. Compensation Strategies
    In this section students explore a range of strategies available to them when they lack a word or phrase that they need to use.

6. Memory Strategies
    The purpose of this section is to stress the need to use newly acquired
    vocabulary. Students discuss both the memory strategies that they
    currently use and some new strategies. They are then given ten newly
    acquired items which they must incorporate while telling a story.
    Students choose the words at random from a group of words, some
    familiar and some unfamiliar. The words may be ones the students
    have recently learned. This strategy enables learners to link, remem-
    ber and use new vocabulary.

7. Practice Strategies
    The aim of this section is to widen the types of practice the students
    use and to focus on different methods of practising language and the
    purposes of these methods. Students compare the strategies they have
    previously employed. Individuals then discuss which of the new strat-
    egies that have emerged would be most useful for them. They then
    select some practice strategies to use.

8. Becoming Familiar with the Speaking Materials
    This section familiarizes students with the speaking materials available
    at the Centre and with their layout and organization. Students look at
    different speaking materials and fill in a chart. They consider the aim
    of the materials; the location of different pieces of information, such
    as level; whether there is a 'map' of the book and, if so, what it con-
    tains; tapescripts and so on. The section emphasizes the focus on flu-
    ency which many materials have while at the same time showing how
    other elements, such as grammar and functions, are included.

9. Planning and Evaluating Your Learning
    The aim of this section is to stress the importance of planning and
    organizing learning, and to help students determine goals and objec-
    tives and the amount of time required to achieve them. Learners
    discuss goals and objectives and fill in a Learner Contract. They then
    look at self- and peer-evaluation; and complete a practice activity.
    Monitoring activities are also discussed.

10. Affective Strategies
    This section helps students explore how their attitudes and emotions
    can affect the learning process and discusses ways of building confi-
    dence. The discussion provides students with an opportunity to con-
    sider their previous language learning problems and how to deal with
    them, as well as ways of becoming more confident.

The Pilot Programme

Participation in the course was voluntary. The learners were highly motivated students who were already attending Summer Programmes at the Study-Centre and who were interested in piloting this module.

There were three groups of learners: Group 1 consisted of three male postgraduate students from China, Group 2 consisted of two female undergraduate students (one had to leave half-way through, her place was taken by another female student who completed the evaluation), and Group 3 consisted of three male undergraduate students.

The course took between ten and twelve hours and groups booked in at their convenience. The first two groups followed the learner training programme in conjunction with a regular Summer Programme, while the third group completed their regular programme first.

EVALUATION AND FUTURE MODIFICATIONS

Evaluation

Feedback from the course was very positive. It was gathered in two forms. Firstly, students were asked to rate the effectiveness of each of the course components (Table 1), secondly, students were asked to comment verbally on the course. One clear outcome of the latter was that all students stated an interest in undertaking further learner training. Elements of the course which participants found particularly useful were sentence stress, word stress, and the memory strategy. Other elements were highlighted by individuals but no particular trends can be identified. Elements which participants found less useful were familiarization with the speaking materials, features of connected speech and differences between listening and speaking.

Many of the participants would have preferred a longer course, in order to have more time to practise. There was less agreement over the timing of the course. One group would have preferred a more intensive course whereas another would have preferred the course to be interspersed with their regular Summer Programme. It should be emphasized that, owing to the very small number of students, the above data can only be considered as indicating possible trends.

Future Modifications

Student feedback will lead to modification of the practice activities for features of connected speech and a practice activity for intonation will be introduced. In addition, the section on materials evaluation will be changed and further suggestions for practising strategies will be made available for

**Table 1   Learning to Learn Speaking Module:
Student Evaluation of Usefulness of Elements of the Module**

	1 (not useful)	2	3	4	5 (very useful)
Aspects of Pronunciation					
Sounds	-	-	3	4	-
Word stress	-	-	2	-	5
Sentence stress	-	-	-	2	5
Features of connected speech	-	1	1	5	-
Intonation	-	1	-	4	2
Becoming familiar with pronunciation materials	-	1	2	3	1
Differences Between Spoken and Written English					
Communication strategies	-	-	1	1	4
Compensation strategies	-	-	-	4	3
Memory Strategies	-	-	1	2	4
Ways of Practising					
Inside the study-centre	-	-	-	1	7
outside the study-centre	-	-	2	1	5
Metacognitive Strategies					
Planning your learning	-	-	1	3	4
Setting goals	-	-	1	4	3
Monitoring your performance	-	-	2	3	2
Evaluating your own and peers' performance	-	-	2	4	2
Affective Strategies					
Considering yourself	-	1	5	2	-
Building confidence	-	-	2	4	2

Note: sections 1-3 were evaluated by seven participants and the other sections by eight participants.

students who want further practice. Finally, an evaluation of each session will be introduced so that students' initial reactions can be gauged at the end of a session.

The strategy questionnaire worked only partially as intended. It worked well to start off an initial discussion and to find out what strategies the learners were familiar with; however, the results show no changes in strategy use. This is probably because only two statements for each of the six types of strategies were used whereas Oxford's SILL test is very comprehensive. If students had developed their use of strategies in general, but had not changed within the specific areas covered by the statements, the development would not be apparent.

In addition, the period between administering the first and second questionnaires (approximately five weeks) was too short. All future learners will complete the full SILL test before they undertake any learner training, then use modified versions for each module, adapted to the skill or area in question, to initiate discussion. Finally, when they are ready to leave the Study-Centre programme, the full SILL test will be re-administered.

CONCLUSION

From the pilot study we can tentatively conclude that the speaking skills module has benefited the learners. They felt it was valuable and were interested in undertaking additional learner training. They showed that they had understood the importance of practice and nearly all requested further practice of the strategies introduced. In addition, all the students in the pilot programme expressed an interest in coming to the Study-Centre to study independently; it therefore appears that they have developed some confidence in independent learning.

The encouraging results achieved with the pilot study of this speaking skills module has led the English Language Study-Centre to commit itself to developing modules in other areas such as listening, grammar and vocabulary each of which will be accompanied by a module-specific Strategies Questionnaire.

REFERENCES

Ellis, G. and Sinclair, B. 1989. *Learning to Learn English*. Cambridge: Cambridge University Press.

Lai, E. and Mak, L. 1992. 'A preliminary report on students' attitudes towards the ILC'. *Occasional Papers in ELT*:1–18. The Chinese University of Hong Kong.

O'Malley, J.M. and Chamot, A.U. 1990. *Learning Strategies in Second Language Acquisition*. Cambridge: Cambridge University Press.

Oxford, R. 1990. *Language Learning Strategies: What Every Teacher Should Know*. Boston: Heinle and Heinle.

CHAPTER 9

Developing Pronunciation Skills through Self-Access Learning

Pamela Rogerson-Revell and Lindsay Miller, Department of English, City Polytechnic of Hong Kong

INTRODUCTION

Interest continues to grow in creating materials to promote independent learning and in developing self-access centres (SAC). There are many examples of successful SACs around the world (Harding-Esch 1982; Dickinson 1987; Riley et al. 1989; Sheerin 1989; Miller 1992). The decision of what type of system to use in the SAC (Miller and Rogerson-Revell 1993) will determine the type of material and the way in which the material is classified, organized and presented for the learner to use. With the receptive skills: reading and listening there are fewer problems in developing and organizing the material than there are with the productive skills: speaking and writing. This paper looks at some of the considerations that have to be made in helping learners to develop their pronunciation skills through self-access.

This paper first clarifies what is meant by 'pronunciation' and gives some brief background to the development of pronunciation teaching and learning. Then it describes some materials and activities for the development of pronunciation learning strategies and provides a guide to some of the most popular pronunciation teaching materials. Finally, some recommendations are made for setting up pronunciation in a SAC.

DEFINING TERMS

In this paper 'pronunciation' is used to refer to a broad range of phonological features including segmentals, suprasegmentals and voice quality features which are also referred to as voice-setting features (Pennington and Richards 1986), voice quality settings (Laver 1980) and paralinguistic features (Brown 1977).

BACKGROUND TO PRONUNCIATION TEACHING

From the 1940s to the mid 1960s, pronunciation teaching was considered an important component of English language teaching, both through the audio-lingual and the situational teaching methodologies. Pronunciation teaching emphasized accuracy at the segmental level, for example, minimal pairs practice and the repetition of controlled dialogues.

During the 1970s, with the development of the 'communicative' approach, pronunciation teaching went out of favour, partly because the emphasis shifted to 'communication' rather than accuracy, and partly because teachers no longer knew how to teach pronunciation as part of communicative language learning.

The 1980s saw a growth of research showing the significance of pronunciation as a tool for communication, particularly at the level of interaction (Brown and Yule 1983).

Currently, there seems to be a growing awareness by teachers and materials writers of the importance of pronunciation and this has led to a renewed interest in this area. However, there seems to have been little systematic attempt to promote a holistic, 'top-down' approach to pronunciation teaching; judging from the majority of current materials available. For example, even seemingly 'communicative' courses like the Headway Pronunciation series (Bowler and Cunningham 1991), although containing some useful exercises on stress, rhythm and intonation, are still predominantly 'segmental' in their approach.

There has now been a shift towards learner-centredness in language teaching and learning which emphasizes the role of the learner as active participant rather than passive recipient. This trend, together with the renewed interest in pronunciation has led to an interest in how pronunciation skills can be developed through independent learning strategies.

MATERIALS AND ACTIVITIES

This section looks at some of the considerations that have to be made when developing pronunciation materials and activities for self-access.

Pronunciation learning strategies exist at different levels, these are: awareness, explanation, recognition, production, and self-correction.

The first task is to raise learners' awareness of how pronunciation affects communication. Pronunciation can affect communication at two levels: global and specific. The global level is when the learner is aware that people speak English differently in different situations. The specific level is when the learner is consciously aware of the particular type of errors that can be made at both the segmental and prosodic levels.

We can begin to sensitize learners to the importance of good pronunciation by encouraging them to make decisions about the steps they will take to overcome pronunciation difficulties they may have (Fig. 1).

Ellis and Sinclair (1989) and Kenworthy (1987) are two sources from which to gather ideas about the type of questions that could go into a general pronunciation questionnaire. Figure 2 is a short example of such a questionnaire.

As can be seen from the questionnaire, the first three questions deal with pronunciation at the segmental level, the next three ask questions about pronunciation at the suprasegmental level, while the last three prompt the learner to think about when they use English.

The next stage in the process of sensitizing the learner to pronunciation is a test. Two types of tests are suggested, one receptive to see if the

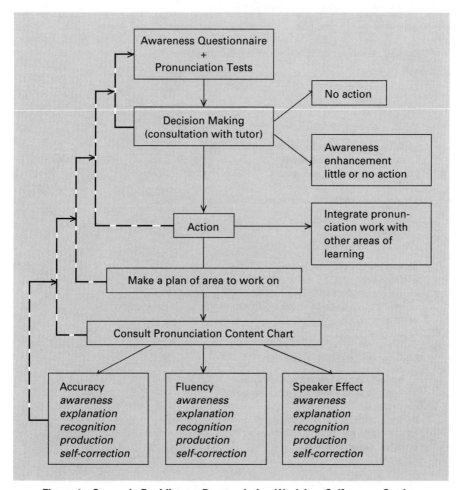

Figure 1   Stages in Deciding on Pronunciation Work in a Self-access Setting

1. How well do you feel you pronounce words in English?

   very well   not bad   O.K.   poorly

2. Do you ever have problems pronouncing words in English?

   Yes   often   ☐   No
         sometimes   ☐
         occasionally   ☐

3. Do you have any of the following problems when pronouncing words in English?

                                                    Yes   No
   difference between two sounds, e.g. /v/ /w/   ☐   ☐
   can't hear the ending of words   ☐   ☐
   can't say the word when I see it written   ☐   ☐
   for the first time

4. How well do you feel you speak English?

   very well   not bad   O.K.   poorly

5. Do you ever hesitate when speaking spontaneously?

   Yes   often   ☐   No
         sometimes   ☐
         rarely   ☐

6. What problems do you have when speaking in English?

   I can't put the words together quickly   ☐
   I can't say long words easily   ☐
   I can't express my feelings well   ☐

7. Do you feel confidant when speaking in English?

   always   sometimes   never

8. Who do you speak English with?

   a) friends/colleagues
   b) teachers
   c) native English speaking foreigners, e.g. Americans
   d) non-native English speaking foreigners, e.g. Singaporians
   e) others, e.g. _____
   f) no one

9. When do you speak English?

   a) socially when talking with friends
   b) socially when talking with strangers
   c) in class
   d) for business, e.g. negotiations, on the telephone
   e) for work, e.g. giving information
   f) other situations, e.g. _____
   g) never

Figure 2   The Pronunciation Questionnaire

learner can differentiate between sounds and prosodic features of speech, and a second to test if the student can produce the appropriate sound contrasts and prosodic features. Examples of the type of sections that need to go into such tests are given below:

Receptive test

Name:..   Date:...................................

The purpose of this test is to find out which parts of English pronunciation may interfere with the way you understand spoken English. How you **hear** English is closely connected with how you **speak** English.

This test is recorded on tape.

A.
How many syllables (beats) are there in these words?
Example:
beauty = 2 (beau-ty)
beautiful = 3 (beaut-ti-ful)

Now listen and write down the number of syllables you hear in each word. You will hear each word twice.

1.	open	....	4. closed	....
2.	difficult	....	5. variation	....
3.	taxes	....		

E.
Is the rhythm of these phrases the same or different? Listen to this example:

. _ .   _   . _ . _

Trafalgar Square   a cup of tea (same)

Now listen and decide if the rhythm of the phrases on the left is the **same** (write S) or **different** (write D) from the phrases on the right. You will hear each phrase once.

1.	Oxford Circus	please be quiet	....
2.	Richmond Road	hurry up	....
3.	Victoria Station	a cup of tea	....
4.	Leicster Square	answer the phone	....
5.	Pall Mall	sit down	....

I.
The movement of your voice (pitch) can change the interpretation of sentences. Can you interpret the meaning of these sentences?
Example:
It was awful.   (statement)
It was awful.   (question)

Now listen to these sentences. Underline one or two words or phrases in brackets that best interprets the meaning of each sentence. You will hear each sentence twice.

1. She left her glasses   (question/statement)
2. He's finished   (question/statement)
3. The number is 35547   (statement/contradiction)
4. It's 22 Hills Road   (statement/contradiction)
5. You're English, aren't you?   (fairly sure/not very sure)
6. That's his sister, isn't it? (fairly sure/not very sure)
7. Really   (very interested/not very interested)
8. Thanks   (very interested/not very interested)
9. I like the garden   (enthusiastic/not very enthusiastic)
10. The kitchen is nice   (enthusiastic/not very enthusiastic)

[Taken from: *Speaking Clearly*, Rogerson and Gilbert 1984]

Production Test

Name:...   Date:...................................

How you say something may affect the clarity of your speech or how the listener understands you. Listen to the words and phrases on the tape and try to say them exactly the same.

Part A: Accuracy

1. Vowels
    a) It's just a flash in the pan.
    b) That band drives me round the bend.
    c) Do you feel ill?
    d) He cut himself on the car door.
    e) If I wait at the gate I'll get wet in the rain.

Part B: Fluency

8. Linking
   a) Is he busy?
   b) May I ask a question?
   c) Can I open a window?
   d) You ought to offer him a job.
   e) Did Ian get caught in the rush hour?

10. Focus
   a) A: What do you do?
      B: I'm a lawyer. What do you do?
   b) A: So, that's 829321.
      B: No, sorry, it's 829341.
   c) A: How was Japan?
      B: I didn't go to Japan, I went to Taiwan.
      A: I thought you were going to Japan.

Once learners have completed the awareness questionnaire and done the pronunciation tests, they have to make some decisions about what, if any, work they are going to do on pronunciation. This decision making could be done by the learners themselves but it is preferable that a self-access tutor or classroom teacher spend some time with each learner and work out a plan of action.

Figure 1 shows that the first decision to be made is whether or not to do anything about pronunciation. Learners may be entirely happy with their pronunciation skills and be aware of the effect pronunciation has on communication. In this case no action need be taken. Or, learners may be happy with their pronunciation skills but be interested in listening out for any weaknesses they may have for future improvement work. On the other hand, learners may decide that they would like to do some pronunciation improvement. Here, again, learners have a choice to make. If the pronunciation weaknesses do not hinder communication then they may decide not to work specifically on any one area of pronunciation, but rather integrate pronunciation work into other areas of language improvement, for example, if they are reading a text they might decide to look up the pronunciation of some new words in a pronunciation dictionary (see *English Pronunciation Dictionary* 1992, or *Longman Pronunciation Dictionary* 1992). Listening is another area where pronunciation work can easily be done, for instance, listening to a dictation and shadowing the speaker. The other option learners have is to do some specific pronunciation work.

If learners decide to work on their pronunciation skills they should then, along with their tutor, consult a pronunciation content chart. This chart will be specially designed by the self-access tutors to reflect the areas that students using a specific self-access centre will need or want help in. An example of a pronunciation content chart is given below:

Questions	Area of work	Worksheet
1–3	**ACCURACY**	
	problem sound contrasts (vowels)	SC 24
	problem sound contrasts (consonants)	SC 23
	/s/ /z/ /ɪz/	H 1
	/v/ /w/	H 2
	/iː/ /ɪ/	H 6
	/l/ /r/	SS 46–49
	syllable stress	SC 2
	word stress	SC 4
	etc.	
4–6	**FLUENCY**	
	understanding accents	tape xx21
	connected speech:	
	rhythm	SC 24
	reductions/contractions	EP 102–31
	linking	EP 76–101
	sentence stress	SC 28
	Intonation:	
	pitch range	B 7&8
	pitch movement	B 2&3
	etc.	
4–9	**VOICE CONTROL**	
	Showing surprise	H 1
	Sounding enthusiastic	H 2
	Showing interest	H 3
	Showing politeness	H 4
	Impact: volume/speed	Video N1
	etc.	
7–9	**SITUATIONS**	
	Social — keeping a conversation going	Video English
	Business — negotiations	Business Assign
	Work — giving instructions	Beyond 2000
	Classroom — presenting information	Video P12

The above pronunciation content chart is only an example, more information and references to worksheets would be necessary. The chart should be placed on the wall of the SAC so that learners could gain easy access to it.

Although the pronunciation content chart suggests published material, some pronunciation books do not follow the path of awareness, explanation, recognition, production, and self-correction mentioned earlier. A decision would need to be made whether to use published material which might be slightly inadequate for self-access learning, or whether teachers should produce their own. The following is an example of the type of pronunciation worksheet that would be of use to learners in a SAC.

Worksheet 16. Basic Sentence Stress

Awareness:
English is based not only on word stress (see worksheet 2 for word stress) but also on sentence stress. Both word stress and sentence stress are important for intelligibility, i.e. how well the listener can understand what you say.

Listen to the following sentence said in different ways. Try to decide which ways of saying the sentence are acceptable, and what the meaning is.

Tape: *The class will start at ten a.m. on Monday the 22nd.*

[This sentence will be recorded on tape several times with the sentence stress changed each time]

Explanation:
In most sentences there are two types of words: content words and structure words. Content words normally carry the most information. Look at this telex message:

SEND MONEY BOUGHT COMPUTER

This is not a complete sentence, but the words carry the important information; they are all content words. Content words are usually emphasized. We can expand the message:

SEND me MONEY I've BOUGHT a COMPUTER

And further:

Please SEND me some MONEY because I've BOUGHT a new COMPUTER.

The words in CAPITALS are content words, the others are structure words. Structure words do not carry so much information. They are not normally emphasized.

Recognition:
Exercise A.
Listen and then underline the content words in the following sentences.
1. Can I have a cup of tea and a piece of cake, please?
2. Thanks for the present.
3. Can I get you another drink?
4. I usually get up late on Saturday.
5. I've never been to Macau.

Production:
Exercise D.
Look at these telex messages and see if you can expand them into complete sentences. Record the sentences onto your tape.

Example: SEND LETTER AIRMAIL
           'Could you SEND the LETTER by AIRMAIL?'

1. CONFIRM ARRIVAL TUESDAY.
2. PLEASE CONTACT. URGENT MESSAGE.
3. ARRANGE TRANSPORT AIRPORT MONDAY.
4. MEETING POSTPONED. CANCEL ROOM.

Self-correction:
Follow-up
Find a partner who will work with you.
     Go to the SPEAKING section and find a topic you would both like to discuss [The learners can be directed to a specific topic, say, giving and receiving information, where sentence stress is important].
     Prepare a cassette to *record* your discussion.
     Record your discussion on tape for about five minutes.
     Stop talking to your partner and listen to the tape. Grade yourself and your partner 'acceptable' or 'not acceptable'. Let your partner listen to the tape and ask him/her to grade both of you. If you disagree on the grading begin the discussion again concentrating on your pronunciation, stop after a few minutes and listen to the playback. Once you are both happy with the *sound* of the discussion continue with the topic stopping each few minutes to listen and grade yourself.
     Once you finish your discussion listen to the tape again. If you feel that you still have problems with the area of pronunciation you are

working on, go back to the worksheet and try some of the exercises again, or ask the self-access tutor for help.

Progress Charts

As part of the ongoing process of self-monitoring, which must be a feature of any self-access system, keeping track of students' pronunciation progress is important. There are several ways to do this:

Written record.   Learners may be encouraged to keep a written record of the activities and materials used in the SAC. As a part of this record, learners may write comments to remind themselves and/or inform the self-access tutor of areas that they are having problems with, or when they feel they have successfully mastered an area.

Audio-taped record.   As part of the induction into using a SAC learners may be required to record a piece of scripted speech and a piece of natural speech. At various intervals while using the SAC learners can tape more samples of their speech and check by themselves or with the tutor whether or not there is any improvement.

Video record.   If the facilities exist, learners could make a video recording of, say, a short oral presentation. Paralinguistic features along with the phonological aspects of the talk could then be analysed and any problems identified. After learners have done some work on the problem areas, another video could be made of the same presentation and the two compared.

Personal monitoring.   If learners are using the SAC regularly and if there is sufficient help available, it may be possible to establish a feedback session when individual learners get together with a tutor and report on their performance in tutorials of the previous day/week. The learners would be required to self-monitor themselves and make decisions about the success of their speech in a particular situation.

PRONUNCIATION BOOKS FOR SELF-ACCESS

Some of the most popular books currently used for teaching pronunciation have been assessed for their usefulness for learners in a SAC. The findings are summarized in Table 1.

Table 1   Pronunciation Books for Use in Self-Access Centres

Title Author Publisher	Supp	L	T B	K	T	S A C	Content	Comments
Headway Pronunciation Bowler and Cunningham OUP	Aud. 3 per level	E PI I UI	✓	✓	×	a	sound contrasts to intonation	- good communicative activities - use with Headway coursebook - not systematic - emphasis on segmentals
Sounds English O'Connor and Fletcher Longman	none	I	×	✓	×	a	mainly minimal pairs exs.	- Intro. for independent learners - lang. chart for 15 lang. groups - tradition layout - no self-correction - not systematic
Intonation in Context Bradford CUP	Aud.	UI to A	✓	✓	×	a	stree and intonation	- systematic (content and structure) - commun. tasks - not very visual - not very 'user-friendly'
Elements of Pronunciation Mortimer CUP	Aud. (4)	I to A	×	×	×	✓	Clusters linking weak forms word and sentence stress	- humorous classification - natural dialogues - well organized - very culture bound - vocab level advanced - not holistic
Ship or Sheep Baker CUP	Aud.	E to I	×	✓	✓	a	minimal pairs	- list of likely errors by nationals - diagnostic test - clear layout - no sensitization - no self-correction - no free production - vocab distracts
Clear Speech Gilbert CUP (US)	Aud.	E to	✓	✓	✓	a	sound contrasts intonation and listening comp	- systematic - useful TB - top-down approach - tests - few comm activities - aimed at TOEFL learners
Pronunciation Plus various contributors MacEnglish (US)	CD	E to I	✓	✓	✓	a	minimal pairs	- visually attractive - sound graphics - very self centred - only minimal pairs - aimed at Japanese market - little comm work

KEY: TB = Teacher's Book,   K = Answer Key,   T = Tests   Aud. = audio cassette,
L = Level,   E = Elementary,   PI = Pre-intermediate,   I = Intermediate,
UI = Upper Intermediate,   A = Advanced,   Supp. = Supplementary material
available,   SAC = suitable for a self-access centre,   a = adaptable

RECOMMENDATIONS

The following factors should be taken into consideration when planning pronunciation training within a SAC environment.

Pronunciation training should be:

1. *Systematic* — as with grammar, it should be clear that the parts belong to a whole system and are interrelated (e.g. rhythm, stress, vowel reduction and vowel lengthening are all related).
2. *Integrated* — it should be linked to other areas of language learning (e.g. vocabulary, grammar, listening, reading), because:
   a) a 'little and often' approach may be more beneficial than spending long periods solely on pronunciation;
   b) showing links with other areas should emphasize the communicative value of pronunciation.
3. *Effective* — it should be seen to have a positive effect on communication, i.e. it should have 'communicative value' in terms of the 'interactional' or 'referential' functions of pronunciation (which enforces the argument for No. 2 above). It should also have clearly defined, and achievable goals.
4. *Global to specific* — it should follow a holistic, 'top-down' approach rather than a 'bottom -up' approach, unlike many published materials which still concentrate largely on segmental features (e.g. Headway Pronunciation series, OUP; Sounds English, Longman).
5. *Controlled* — it should move carefully from controlled to free performance and through the stages: awareness, explanation, recognition, production, and self-correction.
6. *Motivating* — it should be relevant, interesting and credible, i.e. the materials and activities should fit the language level, needs and interests of the learner (unlike some published materials which seem to assume a level of intelligence to match the level of pronunciation, e.g. Baker [1977]).

CONCLUSION

This paper shows examples of the type of considerations that need to be made when preparing learners and developing materials and activities to promote pronunciation within a SAC setting. Establishing a SAC does not automatically mean that learners will become involved in their own language learning, this type of learning has to be actively shaped. The process of awareness, explanation, recognition, production, and self-correction is proposed as a model to follow when developing self-access pronunciation materials and activities.

By carefully planning pronunciation materials and activities in a SAC we can get our learners to recognize the need for changes in their speech pattern, and hopefully give them a sense of self-accomplishment as they improve.

REFERENCES

Baker, A. 1977. *Ship or Sheep*. Cambridge: Cambridge University Press.

Bradford, B. 1988. *Intonation in Context*. Cambridge: Cambridge University Press.

Brown, G. 1977. *Listening to Spoken English*. London: Longman.

Brown, G. and Yule, G. 1983. *Teaching the Spoken Language*. Cambridge: Cambridge University Press.

Bowler, B. and Cunningham, S. 1991. *Headway: Pronunciation*. Oxford: Oxford University Press.

Dickinson, L. 1987. *Self-Instruction in Language Learning*. Cambridge: Cambridge University Press.

Ellis, G. and Sinclair, B. 1989. *Learning to Learn English*. Cambridge: Cambridge University Press.

English Pronunciation Dictionary. 1992. Cambridge: Cambridge University Press.

Gilbert, J. B. 1984. *Clear Speech*. New York. Cambridge University Press.

Harding-Esch, E. 1982. 'The Open Access Sound and Video Library of the University of Cambridge. Progress report and development'. *System* 10(1):13–28.

Kenworthy, J. 1987. *Teaching English Pronunciation*. London: Longman.

Laver, J. 1980. *The Phonetic Description of Voice Quality*. Cambridge: Cambridge University Press.

Longman Pronunciation Dictionary. 1992. London: Longman.

Miller, L. 1992. *Self-Access Centres in S.E. Asia*. Hong Kong: Research Report No. 11. Department of English, City Polytechnic of Hong Kong.

Miller, L. and Rogerson-Revell, P. 1993. 'Self-access systems'. *ELT Journal* 47(3):228–33.

Mortimer, C. 1985. *Elements of Pronunciation*. Cambridge: Cambridge University Press.

O'Connor, J. D. and Fletcher, C. 1989. *Sounds English*. Harlow: Longman.

Pennington, M. and Richards, J. 1986. 'Pronunciation revisited'. *TESOL Quarterly* 20(2):207–26.

Pronunciation Plus. 1990. Salt Lake City: MacEnglish.

Riley, P., Gremmo, M. and Moulden, H. 1989. 'Pulling yourself together: the practicalities of setting up and running self-access systems', in D.

Little (ed.) *Self-access Systems for Language Learning*. Dublin: Authentik.

Rogerson, P. and Gilbert, J.B. 1990. *Speaking Clearly*. Cambridge: Cambridge University Press.

Sheerin, S. 1989. *Self Access*. Oxford: Oxford University Press.

Section Three

Materials

CHAPTER 10

Creating Simple Interactive Video for Self-Access

David Gardner, English Centre, The University of Hong Kong

INTRODUCTION

Over the last few years Hong Kong has witnessed a flurry of activity in the area of self-access learning, particularly in relation to the learning of language. While the secondary sector is beginning to show a cautious interest, tertiary institutions have already made major investments of resources, both human and material, as have some non-government sponsored training operations. As self-access centres mature in Hong Kong a problem that they are encountering is the paucity of quality materials which lend themselves well to working in self-access mode. While many publishers have quickly added 'self-access', 'self-study' or 'independent learning' at strategic points in their catalogues, most of their self-access publications are little more than classroom versions with answer keys, and sometimes tapescripts, added.

The availability of video materials for use in self-access is particularly problematic. There is a lot of good quality video teaching material but there is very little that can be described, as it stands, as good quality learning material. This is no surprise when we consider the goals of most of this video material, it was designed to be used by teachers in classrooms. What has typically turned quality teaching material into quality learning material is the teachers' input. If that material is made available for self-access learning without providing, in some way, the teachers' input to go with it, it will be of limited benefit to learners.

Video is an extremely popular medium for self-access language learning. This paper will explore a way of capitalizing on that popularity by changing passive viewers into active, or even interactive, users and by increasing cheaply and quickly the quantity of quality video learning materials.

THE PROBLEMS OF USING VIDEO IN SELF-ACCESS LEARNING

Probably the single greatest practical difficulty in using video is being able to find the right place on the tape. Teachers who use video in class already know about this frustration which they will have experienced when cueing up a tape before going into class. The learner, functioning in a foreign language, can find this problem unsolvable. Some published materials overcome this problem by providing an on-screen counter.

Another problem may be that of selection. For classroom use a teacher may select fifteen minutes from a one-hour tape and spend a lesson working on its language potential. Self-access users might watch the whole hour of tape and not know what to do with it. Of course, in self-access mode users are free to make that choice but they might also choose to work in guided mode if it were made available. Some published courses do provide such guidance although it frequently occurs wholly or partially in the teachers' notes.

A further difficulty associated with using teaching materials in a self-access centre is that of individualizing a classroom resource. In material designed for classroom use it is not uncommon for accompanying print materials to contain pair work and group work based around the video. It may also contain very open ended questions designed to stimulate a discussion at which the teacher is always available as a resource to provide information and ultimately answers. While these elements may still be useful in certain self-access activities it is important that users should at least be provided with an alternative way of working in which they can choose to work alone and in which they can check their answers in the absence of a teacher. The simple solution is to provide answer sheets, which many packages do, but these can do little to answer 'discussion questions'. A better solution might be to rewrite the questions.

The greatest problem on a pedagogical level is that many users of video in self-access become passive viewers. The problem of passive viewing of video is one about which we have been being warned for more than a decade (Geddes and Sturtridge 1982; Lonergan 1984; Allen 1985; Cooper et al. 1991). Passive viewers use video the way they might watch television at home, that is, they allow it to wash over them. This use of self-access video for language immersion is one useful role but there is potential for other roles. With teacher directed classroom use of video opportunities are provided for active viewing activities which lead to focused language learning. Such activities should also be available to self-access users but frequently are not.

The use of published material not specifically aimed at the ELT market can compound the problems. Materials such as documentaries originally made for television use, open learning materials on a diversity of topics, plays, promotional tapes and video films can all be seen as useful learning resources. These materials, however, have no on-screen counter, no learner guidance notes and no answer keys (usually because there are no questions), however, these are often the materials which prove most popular in self-access. With better pedagogical support these materials could contribute greatly to helping self-access learners reach their goals.

SOLUTIONS

Self-access is proving that it has an important role to play in language learning in Hong Kong. To maintain its position, however, a wide range of materials must be made available. Quantity as well as quality is important if true independent learning is to be encouraged. The key to increasing quantity is to solve the problems highlighted above.

More Teachers

It may be felt that the solution to problems caused by students working alone is to provide more teachers who would offer more learner support in self-access centres. This would overcome the problem of using video (and other) materials which are not totally suited to self-access use. Teachers, or facilitators, would be on hand to teach the bits that are missing in the materials just like they do in the classroom.

This is an obviously unworkable solution. Self-access centres need facilitators and they need to be well qualified teachers who are able to guide students, initiate learning activities and produce quality materials. However, to provide facilitators who also take on the role of classroom teacher but on a one-to-one basis is financial suicide. Diverting more teachers into the self-access area, even on a temporary basis, is only a good solution to this problem if its purpose is to increase the availability of materials, not if it is to increase the availability of teachers.

Materials Development

A second solution to the problem of finding quality video material for self-access is to use some of the resources being pumped into self-access centres to provide staff time to develop suitable new materials. This is a solution that has already been 'discovered' in Hong Kong and there are currently discussions going on about (and searching out funding for) a number of projects which will involve the production of video materials relevant to the needs of students in Hong Kong. These projects will provide good quality video material containing characters our students can identify with and situations and places they know. This material might then be made available on videotape and videodisc, it might also be accompanied by print materials and/or be turned into a multimedia package.

Such projects are to be welcomed because they will provide good quality, attractive video which will be useable not only in self-access centres but also in the classroom. However, these projects are insignificant in terms of our current self-access needs. They will provide a small amount of untested material, probably with highly focused ESP objectives. The project cost will be extremely high. The delivery date will be at some, as yet unknown, point in the future (but realistically a minimum of two years). The self-access centres of Hong Kong need to provide learners with an extensive range of materials and they need to do it now.

Materials Adaptation

A lower key, lower budget solution to materials development is to adapt materials that have been tried and tested in the classroom. This is something of a compromise but adapting materials to meet new needs is something with which many language teachers are already familiar. A great advantage is that the materials selected have already been tried and tested in the classroom. Already in Hong Kong a number of projects have been successful in adapting course materials from major ELT publishers for use in self-access (Gardner 1993a). Adaptations involving video material can encounter some or all of the problems mentioned above; learners have difficulty finding the right part of the tape, if they find it they are not always sure what to do with it, essential teacher input may be lacking and so on.

An effective way of overcoming the problems of adapting video for self-access use is to place it under computer control. A computer can be interfaced with a video playback system and programmed to find relevant video segments easily. It can also be used to provide instructions and information, ask and answer questions, offer users choices about what they want to do and how they want to progress as well as monitoring user progress, giving feedback and even running tests on the material if required. The disadvantage of such learning material is that it can become time consuming to design and may need specialist input to write computer programs and to solve technical problems. This, in turn, can make it an expensive solution. The criteria for a simple interactive video system to solve the current problems of using video in self-access centres are that it can offer easy access to any part of a videotape and that it can allow information, instructions, questions and answers to be integrated with the video. Most importantly, it must be a system that can be used by teachers rather than technologists.

A SIMPLE INTERACTIVE VIDEO SYSTEM

The criteria for a simple interactive video system are met by the aXcess system[1] (Lambert and Hart 1991), a hardware and software solution which is currently in use at the University of Hong Kong and is on trial at the Vocational Training Council and the Open Learning Institute. A recent research project run jointly by the English Centre and the Centre for Media Resources of the University of Hong Kong (Gardner 1993b; Hart 1993) showed it to be a useful developmental platform, simple and relatively quick to work with and popular with student users.

The system consists of a one piece unit which contains a video playback system permanently interfaced with a PC compatible computer. The video screen is used to show the computer display or video when it is playing. A normal computer keyboard is used for student input although the system can be adapted to accept other input devices. The system can be used as a video player only or as a computer controlled video player.

The system uses what is normally the second audio channel of the video as a timecode track. This allows it to be absolutely frame accurate. Each frame of the video has a unique number which can be used as a start or stop point for playing a segment of video. These numbers are incorporated into a computer program which controls when and how the segments are accessed and what happens on the computer screen before and after the video is played. The control program can be a simple tape management program or it can include instructional material with which the user interacts.

This system is sufficiently simple for teachers to manage without input from technologists. The software package consists of utilities to facilitate screen design and collection of timecode numbers. The language with which control programs are written consists of a total of only forty commands. A simple program could be written using less than half of these. In a recent experiment three teachers who were computer literate but with no knowledge of programming and no previous experience of working with video, learned the system during the course of a 15-hour workshop. In a further six hours, working as a team, they had produced a small working program. This time included every step of the process and with experience could be cut to four or perhaps three hours.

Length of program development time is variable as it depends on the quantity of learner material being produced and the complexity of the program being developed. The advantage of a system which is in the hands of teachers is that they are able to make all the decisions. Teachers can decide how much time to invest, what they want the outcome to be, which tapes to use and what the instructional and informational content of the program should be. In expensive interactive video packages these decisions have already been made and often do not suit the needs of our learners.

INTERACTIVE VIDEOTAPE VERSUS INTERACTIVE VIDEODISC

Inevitably, interactive videotape systems get compared with interactive videodisc systems. By comparison videotape systems are slow (in both video and computer processing), unsophisticated, do not have colour graphics or overlay of text on the video screen and are unable to make use of artificial intelligence in their user interface. This comparison is irrelevant because like is not being compared with like. However, if we are to make the comparison we should also note that videodisc systems:
- are vastly more expensive,
- do not provide computer and video in one integral unit,
- use hardware that requires a greater level of technical support,
- can only make use of videodisc (the stock of which is minuscule compared to videotape and which is not always easy to obtain),
- cannot easily also be used in the classroom,
- often operate custom-built software which ranges from not relevant to our students to appallingly full of mistakes,
- use software which cannot be adapted by local teachers,
- use software packages which may vary in their requirements for specific hardware peripherals and setups,
- cannot easily be programed without programming experience,
- require anything up to 500 hours of programmer's time for one hour of learner time for those who want to produce their own materials.

ADVANTAGES OF A TAPE-BASED SYSTEM

Both videotape-based and videodisc-based systems have their advantages and disadvantages but they are not comparable. Self-access centres are likely to want to invest in both systems to provide the widest range of facilities for their users. If we accept that a videotape-based system should

be assessed in its own right we need to look at what it can offer self-access learning:
- there are large quantities of good video already available,
- teachers have been using videotape for years and they know how best to adapt it for students use,
- tapes provided in self-access can also be used in the classroom,
- materials preparation is relatively quick and easy,
- preparation can be undertaken by teachers,
- materials can be easily edited,
- the software and hardware will always be compatible.

Computer control offers the opportunity to convert passive video viewers into active video users. However, this can only happen on a simple system that is easy enough for teachers to learn in the time they have available to them and with the level of expertise they have or are prepared to achieve. Practical considerations need to be taken into account. Teachers' time is limited and usually available in irregular blocks. A simple system is essential if they are to use their time for real development rather than to constantly re-learn a complex system. A tape-based system is simpler, faster and easier to understand but still has enough flexibility to allow teachers to experiment with their approach.

CONCLUSION

The future holds the potential for some good quality, locally focused interactive video teaching materials to become available which will be entirely or partially self-access based. Such materials are eagerly awaited but they will never form more than a small part of the extensive range of video materials that self-access centres should be offering their users.

A more important goal is to find ways of making the vast quantity of video material that already exists more suitable for self-access use. This can be done by using a simple videotape computer control system. This will provide simple tape management facilities for some videotapes and allow teachers to make others more interactive by adding their own instructional content.

Simple systems are a more sensible option for this task than more sophisticated and more complex systems because they allow the work to be managed by teachers not technologists and they restrict the consumption of human and material resources to a minimum. The benefits for learners are on three levels which correspond to the level of work undertaken to adapt the video. At the lowest level, where the computer provides a tape management system, learners avoid the frustration of searching through videotapes. At the next level, where teachers have added some informational and instructional component, the learner changes from a passive viewer to an active learner. At the highest level, where users are offered choices and receive feedback on their input, the learning becomes interactive.

NOTE

1. The aXcess Video System was developed by Canberra Professional Equipment in Australia.

REFERENCES

Allan, M. 1985. *Teaching English with Video*. Essex: Longman.

Cooper, R., Lavery, M. and Rinvolucri, M. 1991. *Video*. Oxford: Oxford University Press.

Gardner, D. 1993a. 'Copyright, publishers and self-access centres'. *Hong Kong Papers in Linguistics and Language Teaching* 16:111–5.

———. 1993b. 'Interactive video in self-access learning: development issues', in *Interactive Multimedia '93*, Proceedings of the Fifteenth Annual Conference. Washington: Society for Applied Learning Technology.

Geddes, M. and Sturtridge, G. 1982. *Video in the Language Classroom*. London: Heinemann Educational Books.

Hart, I. 1993. 'Interactive video in self-access learning: evaluation issues', in *Interactive Multimedia '93*, Proceedings of the Fifteenth Annual Conference. Washington: Society for Applied Learning Technology.

Lambert, B. and. Hart, I. 1991. 'Interactive videodisc for the rest of us', in *Interactive Instruction Delivery*, Proceedings of the Ninth Annual Conference. Orlando: Society for Applied Learning Technology.

Lonergan, J. 1984. *Video in Language Teaching*; Cambridge: Cambridge University Press.

CHAPTER 11

Materials Production for Self-Access Centres in Secondary Schools

Janice Tibbetts, King's College, Hong Kong

INTRODUCTION

The purpose of this paper is to show how materials can be developed for a self-access system in secondary schools. That such a centre is worthwhile is becoming more and more obvious to teachers in Hong Kong. It can go a long way towards the problem of large, mixed ability classes and free the teacher for more productive work with small groups or individuals. It can provide remedial help for weaker students and challenging material to stretch the high flyers. But setting up such a centre can seem an impossible task. There are major problems in government secondary schools in Hong Kong as there are, no doubt, in schools in other parts of the world. These problems stem from the dire shortage of money to buy in ready made materials and the lack of teachers skilled and experienced in the production of in-house materials. I hope to show how to set about producing appropriate materials without breaking copyright, spending a fortune or hiring a materials writer.

The first and most important point to bear in mind is that one cannot afford to be over ambitious. Having seen what exists in the tertiary sector, one may be tempted to aim for a large air-conditioned room or even rooms filled with all sorts of marvellous resources such as interactive computer and video facilities, listening booths and a wealth of varied and interesting materials for improving reading and writing skills. But that is not the reality of life in an average school. Problems of space and scheduling alone mean that such a facility would never be utilized fully enough to justify the expense even with highly motivated students and enthusiastic teachers. Instead one needs to begin on a much smaller scale, one that is appropriate to the money, space, time, range of skills and expertise available in the school. To do this it is important to have a general idea of the ultimate aim and design of the planned self-access centre (SAC) but to narrow the focus and begin with a very limited range of material in order to train both teachers and learners to handle such a radically different learning style.

SELECTING THE TARGET GROUP

The first step must be to select the target group of learners. This is to ensure that material produced in the early stages of the self-access development programme is not spread thinly over too many different levels. The amount of material required is so vast that it is better to have a lot at one level than a tiny amount at several levels. Students will soon lose interest if they find that they have completed all the material they can cope with and what is left is too easy or too difficult. There is also the question of interest. One of the advantages of self-access learning from the students' point of view is that they can select material that they are interested in and activities that they enjoy. One of the aims of self-access is that it increases student independence and leads them to be self-motivated. If the material is dull or is not within their range of interests then the motivation will be lacking. Given the wide range of different interests there may be in a class of forty plus students, it is obviously important to have as wide a range as possible of topics, writing styles and exercise types.

Selecting the target group establishes the level band of the material in a secondary school. When selecting the level at which to start, it is important to define the aims of the self-access system you plan to set up (Miller and Rogerson-Revell 1993). If the aim is simply to motivate students, to try to help them to get over their fears in learning English and to begin to enjoy learning the language, then the level is of less importance than it is if you are trying to prepare students for the rigours of tertiary study, with its emphasis on private study and research and self-discipline.

In my school our concern is with the older students who are preparing for tertiary education. The reasons for this are as follows. In Hong Kong schools, as in many schools in Asia, the cultural norms and the weight of teaching traditions militate against self-access learning. As a result the introduction of any programme of independent learning requires a lot of teacher and learner training. The older, more mature students will find it easier to study in this way and as they learn, their teachers will also be learning — to let go, to trust the students, to drop the role of teacher as an omniscient, all powerful authoritarian figure in favour of a role as consultant and facilitator in the learning process. To introduce this way of learning to younger students in form one would be much more difficult. It can be done, but in my school we have chosen to do this at a later stage when teachers themselves feel more relaxed and at home with the system. Consequently, we have decided to start with materials for the sixth form, and that is the area that I shall concentrate on in this paper. There are three basic reasons for this:

1. Traditionally sixth form classes are smaller than in the lower forms. Generally there are thirty students instead of the forty-plus of the lower forms. This means that less material is needed and when starting from scratch this is an important consideration.

2. Sixth formers are mature enough to cope with the release from the rigid 'lockstep' control of traditional teaching and yet are less anxious about external examinations than fifth formers, and hence more willing to take a break from the traditional examination preparation techniques of completing endless past papers.

3. Producing material for this level allows for a 'trickle through' effect. The range of abilities means that very advanced material can be produced which will cater for the best in the sixth form and still be suitable for students in year seven, yet material aimed at the less able sixth former can later be used by fifth or even very good fourth formers when the facility is expanded to include them. Done in this way, from higher forms down, the admission to the self-access programme becomes a privilege bestowed on those with maturity to benefit. This is an enormous psychological advantage.

SELECTING THE MAIN FOCUS OF MATERIAL

After deciding on the level of material the next major decision to be made is the main focus of the material. In a school, with its heavy teaching and administrative load, there is little time to spare for materials writing. This is especially true in Hong Kong which, like a number of other Asian countries, lays heavy stress on frequent testing and examinations. Although the final aim should be to develop the self-access facility to cover the whole range of skills and sub-skills, this is not going to be possible immediately. It is therefore vital to decide what type of material to produce. When deciding the focus areas it is not necessary to restrict oneself to any traditional system such as a Library of Congress classification or a traditional E.F.L. 'four skills' approach. It is best to decide on the focus areas your students need help with and describe them in terms that staff and students who will be using the SAC find helpful. Material can be labelled under the headings of skills: reading, writing, listening, speaking, or under the headings of styles or register: English for science, English for study purposes, etc. The nine main focus areas which I believe to be necessary in my school are reading, listening, writing, speaking, vocabulary, grammar, social English, academic English and thinking skills. Some of these may overlap to some extent, for example speaking and English for social purposes. However, the speaking section will include material on pronunciation and intonation, while the social English section will offer help with writing and understanding written forms as in short informal notes, letters and invitations, for instance, as well as teaching 'small talk'. Within the skills area most teachers would agree that the receptive skills of reading and listening are the best ones to begin with as they are easier to deal with than the more active ones of speaking and writing, for a number of reasons, not least being that it is easier for students to check their own work.

We decided to produce material for the first section, reading, because sixth formers aiming towards the Advanced Supplementary examination need to read fast and effectively to achieve success in the examination, especially in the Practical Skills for Work and Study paper. Also, one of the main complaints that we constantly hear from the tertiary sector is that Hong Kong students have not been taught how to read efficiently. This accusation rankles among secondary school teachers, who all know that the students have been taught but the pressures of the syllabus, testing requirements and timetabling do not allow time for the practice of these skills which is essential if they are to be properly assimilated by students. Teaching is only one side of the educational coin; learning is the other, and the fact that a topic has been taught does not necessarily mean that it has been learned. It is here that a self-access facility can be of great value in helping students to learn. It can provide teaching notes to help those who did not understand or were absent when the original lesson was given and who are unable or unwilling to seek the advice of the teacher for various reasons. It can also provide graded practice material for the student to work on alone without increasing the heavy marking load of the teacher. Yet the teacher is available in school if the student requires further explanation.

ORGANIZING THE MATERIALS

Once the focus for materials has been decided the next decision is the approach to adopt in the production and organization of materials. In the case of reading the easiest and most obvious approach is to simply select reading passages by topic, for example, smoking, capital punishment, the environment, etc. — all the hoary old grist of the liberal studies mill — and write general comprehension questions on the passages. This approach will provide plenty of material for the practice of reading skills. However, it is difficult to organize it to provide teaching material and I suggest that for students in Hong Kong something a little more specific is needed, especially for those students who are in difficulties. They need overt guidance on how to improve their ability. I believe it better to concentrate initially on the development of skills rather than to emphasize the content of the material to be included in the centre as in a topic based approach. Of course, that does not prevent the inclusion of material on interesting topics. The best approach is to break down the macro skill, reading, into component micro skills. For the general purposes required in a secondary school the taxonomy given by Grellet (1981:12–3) is perfectly adequate. She divides the subject area into four main areas. These are: reading techniques; how the aim of the writer is conveyed; the understanding of meaning; assessing the text. Each of these areas is further subdivided. The first part, reading techniques, is divided into three main parts: sensitizing; improving reading speed; skimming and scanning. Each of the sub-sections is then broken down further into smaller sections. Sensitizing is broken into three parts: inference of meaning; understanding relations within the sentence; linking. Each one of these is then broken down even further to yield: inference through the context; inference through word formation; and so on.

Clearly for most secondary schools in Hong Kong producing enough materials to cover the whole of the taxonomy suggested would be an extremely long and Herculean task. The solution is therefore to select the micro skills that teachers feel are the most urgently required by the students in their own schools. In my own school, for example, it was felt that students had difficulty in separating the wood from the trees when reading. That is, they tend to focus too much on the specifics, especially the parts they do not understand and they miss the overall meaning which they could understand perfectly well if they would lift their eyes off the problem and look at the whole. This is a very familiar problem which all teachers are constantly bemoaning. We decided to tackle it by producing material to teach very basic reading techniques followed by plenty of material to *practise* these skills. The techniques selected were divided as follows:

1. Word and sentence based
   a. coping with unknown words
      i.   using context
      ii. using knowledge of word formation
   b. coping with long or complicated sentences
2. Text based
   a. skimming texts for a macro view
   b. scanning texts for specific information

This is just the beginning and we plan to widen the range of material covered in the long term but it is plenty for us to cope with in the immediate term. The system I have developed consists of laminated worksheets. Students may use these but may not take them away. Although laminating is fairly expensive, it has a number of advantages.

Firstly providing one laminate is cheaper than providing an individual copy for each student. Secondly, they have a prime advantage in that they can be originals and not photocopies. This is very important because of the problem of copyright. Thirdly, laminates have a longer shelf life. They are less easily torn or dirtied and students cannot deface them easily. Finally, because they are originals and not copies, the quality is of a high standard and it is possible to have attractive worksheets with pictures in colour, which can be quite important in making the material appealing to students.

Laminating offers a way of providing material which is cheap, durable, copyright clean and attractive. The system which I am developing and which I strongly recommend is one in which four types of worksheets are provided. Each one is colour coded to guide the student. They consist of:

- A teaching unit, giving an explanation and lots of examples.
- A reading passage which may be at sentence, paragraph or longer level.
- A practice unit giving questions, or tasks.
- An answer sheet giving not only answers but also full explanations where necessary.

GENERATING MATERIAL

Having decided what material is required the next step is to decide how to generate it. There are three main areas for consideration. These are sourcing material, designing exercises and grading both material and exercises. The first and in my view one of the most important considerations is that of sourcing material. The prime aim has to be to interest students so material must be searched out that will do just that. This is not too difficult if the target group is within the junior levels or if the main focus of the material is vocabulary or grammar games. It becomes more difficult when the target group is senior students and the main focus is to improve reading skills. Three criteria have to be met:

1. What is going to interest students?
2. What is going to be useful to them?
3. What material fits the exercise or skill area?

I have a word of warning here on the first criterion. It is all too easy to fall into the adult trap of thinking we know it all. We don't. And students can surprise us immensely. I have worked on a self-access programme for students from Chinese medium schools who were taking a four week bridging course run by the British Council for the Education Department (see Forrester, this volume). There was a wide range of topics for them to read about and although some were predictably popular, some that one would expect to be very much in demand were ignored while others which seemed less likely to excite interest were snapped up eagerly. The answer to this problem is to seek the help of students when sourcing materials. Get your students to bring in interesting articles from books, magazines and newspapers. Talk to them about their interests, perhaps during one of the self-access lessons and use the information later. However, beware of pitfalls even here. Some of the most popular articles in the self-access centre this summer were those dealing with any aspect of *Jurassic Park*. But if the school is to spend money on laminating materials for the SAC such topicality is not necessarily a good thing. Who will want to read about *Jurassic Park* in two month's time? Who would pick up an article about *Jaws*? The same problem arises with the selection of texts on such passing fancies as pop or film stars. Last year Andy Lau, this year Leon, next year who? If materials are to be used long term, it is important that the texts themselves are usable for a reasonable period. For this reason newspapers are a less useful source than might be expected. Yesterday's newspaper is today's fish wrapper. Magazines provide a more fruitful source, especially if general interest and universal topics are selected. Interesting ephemera can be kept in its original form either in the school library or in the classroom.

On the second criterion, usefulness, there are again a number of factors to bear in mind, the main one being who is the SAC for and what is its primary purpose? In the case of my school, preparing students for tertiary education, texts about pop stars are likely to be quite interesting but of small value in preparing for the Use of English Exam or for tertiary studies, although such articles may be of value in arousing the interest of reluctant readers or in providing light relief after intensive study even in a SAC such as ours.

The next decision is that of the exercise type. Variety is important but for inexperienced materials writers, it is probably easier to stick to one type of exercise at a time, and produce lots of them before going on to produce another type. The system I have adopted is to take one skill area, for example reading, then focus on a sub-skill, such as guessing vocabulary from context. We begin at sentence level, which is the easiest both for teachers to write and for students to read and begin with and we write our own material. One way to tackle this for non-native speakers who feel unsure of their ability is to follow a standard procedure. First, select the vocabulary. When doing this it is important to remember that the words themselves are of less importance than the skill of using context to guess their meaning. A good teacher should have a fair idea of which words an average, weak and top class sixth former will know. It is easy enough to check. Sometimes I just stop students in passing and ask them if they know a word. It is heartening to discover how often my guesses are right. Another technique I have used is to look through texts in books and newspapers that my students have been reading and pick out all the words they have underlined. Another method is to jot down or store in the memory all the vocabulary items which students ask about in the course of a lesson and use it later to produce materials for students who use the SAC.

Having built up a store of vocabulary items the teacher uses a range of dictionaries, to write sentences to illustrate the meanings of the words selected. It is important that sentences illustrate the meaning of the word rather than defining it. For example if the word chosen is 'clink' then the phrase 'a sharp ringing sound' which is the definition given in the Oxford Advanced Learner's Dictionary, Encyclopaedic Edition is not useful for a vocabulary exercise designed to teach the skill of guessing meaning from context. That dictionary gives a phrase to illustrate the meaning 'the clink of coins, keys, glasses.' Again, this is not quite enough for our exercise, both because it is not a complete sentence and because it does not give enough context for an exercise at sentence level, which is the lower level of exercise designed for students for whom this skill is either a new one or one at which they feel themselves to be weak. However, the illustration in the dictionary does give us a starting point. I then take this dictionary phrase or one from another dictionary to write a sentence in which the meaning is very clear. I might then write a sentence such as the following 'In the silent examination hall the clink of coins in the teacher's pocket as he walked between the desks is a noise I shall never forget.' If a team of teachers work on this together, reading and commenting on each other's efforts before anything is finally accepted for lamination then it is possible to produce quite a lot of material in a fairly short time. It can also be an enormous benefit to the teachers themselves who not only have the chance to improve their own skills but also gain experience of working in a team which does not happen as often as it could in Hong Kong schools. From sentence level the next step is to search out paragraphs and short passages which contain some difficult vocabulary but which also give enough con- textual clues to make guessing the meanings fairly simple. As material is added the tasks should become more difficult. This is only one example of how material may be produced. The same graded development and team approach can and should be used for the production of material for a sixth form reading skills, a first year vocabulary enrichment or any other element of a SAC.

SOURCES OF MATERIALS

Acquiring good material for a SAC can seem difficult at first but the sources available are many and varied. It depends, of course what the focus and sub-focus are. If it is the development of reading skills then the possibilities are almost limitless. Feature articles from newspapers rather than pure news, which dates too quickly, can be used, as can articles from a wide variety of magazines, books, travel brochures given away free by travel agencies, advertising leaflets, concert and other performance programmes, and all the myriad publications of our communications age. Acquiring these can be done by simply going round the various agencies and stores but a better way is to write to companies and ask for copies. At the same time one can ask for copying permission. Stores, advertising agencies, commercial and manufacturing companies, airlines and hotels are just a few of the commercial sources for materials. Useful non-commercial sources are government departments, voluntary agencies such as charities and pressure groups, embassies and consulates. Some of these will also give copies of audio and video materials.

Depending on the purpose of your self-access centre you can include commercially bought games such as Scrabble, Word Yahtzee, Call My Bluff or Crossword, or you can make your own games, perhaps with the help of students from the English Club. Popular and successful games that I have used include Grammar Dominoes, Grammar Monopoly, and Grammar Snakes and Ladders. Many excellent books containing ideas for games are available such as Greenall (1983), Rinvolucri (1984), and Hadfield and Hadfield (1990).

Students can provide a lot of materials for a SAC. This is a useful source of materials which is often overlooked. They can provide the raw material by bringing in written or audio material which they like and which interests them. But they can also provide finished exercises. You can exploit students' work in a number of ways.

1. Interesting, well-written stories and essays can be included as general interest reading material. In this case it is important that the writing is not merely of the 'best composition' variety. The story or essay must be on a topic of genuine interest to students and unless it is extremely well written, the Hong Kong certificate style of composition on themes of traffic accidents, jewel shop robberies or the school picnic is very unlikely to arouse interest.

2. Other materials which have interested students in my school include

a) Acrostic poems, lavishly illustrated either by the student authors or by artistic friends.

b) Work inspired by a class reader, especially the spin off style of activity such as a student recorded news broadcast of an event in the story or a word search puzzle using lexical sets from the reader or simply lexical items from certain chapters. These appeal even to classes that are not using that particular reader.

c) Limericks, haiku and other very short poems, especially when composed for a particular event or festival. Valentines and anti-Valentine poems were a huge success as were spells and curses for Halloween.

d) 'Agony aunt'-style letters seeking and giving advice.

e) Suggestions and complaints dealing with the running of various activities in the school.

f) Lyrics produced to fit in to the tunes of well known songs.

3. For more exam oriented students past papers and answer keys can be a valuable resource and I propose that these should include past internal examinations as well as external ones.

4. Another idea for the SAC is to build up topic-based data packs on general knowledge topics that may be the subject of examination. These can include news items but again, if you plan to build up a library resource facility then too much topicality can be a disadvantage. In any case the data files will need regular revision and updating.

CODING AND INDEXING THE SAC MATERIALS

At first the indexing system of the SAC may not seem very important. There may be only a limited amount of material and the teachers and students may find it relatively easy to lay hands on whatever is required. But as the amount of material grows, it becomes increasingly necessary to have a way of organizing it to make it user friendly. I suggest that it is better to have a system in place from the start rather than try to impose one retrospectively. Although existing library classifications such as the Dewey decimal system may seem appropriate, they are not as helpful as they would at first appear for learners of a second or foreign language. It would be another matter, of course, if the SAC were to develop into a truly cross-curricular facility. The system I would recommend is that suggested by Sheerin (1989). As she so rightly points out 'it seems to be human nature to browse' (Sheerin 1989:27) so that card index or microfiche facilities are ignored and the emphasis needs to be laid on careful labelling of the material itself. If this is organized well from the beginning it becomes easier to incorporate new material into the SAC.

LOCATION OF SAC MATERIALS

Deciding where to locate materials is an important factor in establishing a SAC. This is outside the scope of this paper which is really concerned with the production of materials but it is a question which looms large in many schools in Hong Kong which are chronically overcrowded. The solutions are to be found, however, with a little ingenuity. It may be possible, for example, to take over a corner of the library, and to timetable classes in for their self-access lesson. If there is only a small amount of material it may be possible to keep some in a cupboard in each classroom and rotate it between classrooms periodically. Another possibility is to keep a trolley or a cupboard on each floor and take the materials in to the classroom as required. If, as in some schools, classes are located together, with for example first-year students on the ground floor, second and third-year students on the first floor, etc., then this makes the organization of materials easier, although it must be remembered that levels need to be thought of in very broad bands to allow for the wide range of abilities in each form. Thus the box for third formers could include some materials within the capability of good first formers and also suitable for weak fourth or even fifth formers.

CONCLUSION

In this paper I have tried to show how materials may be found and prepared for self-access centres in Hong Kong secondary schools. To summarize, the steps to success are:
- Be constantly on the look-out for possible materials.
- Be willing to ask for outside help where necessary.
- Begin with a clear idea of what the SAC should be like in its final form.
- Start by selecting an initial target group of SAC users.
- Choose the main focus of the material to be produced rather than try to produce a comprehensive range.
- Decide on the organizational approach to the chosen material.
- Form a team to produce materials. (In some schools with non-English specialists teaching English it is possible to have everybody working on the sourcing of materials while the specialist English teachers write the materials and the non-specialists do the cutting, sticking and laminating tasks.)
- Decide on the classification system to be used before any material is put into the SAC.
- Make an early decision on the initial and final location of the SAC materials.

REFERENCES

Grellet, F. 1981. *Developing Reading Skills*. Cambridge: Cambridge University Press.

Greenall, S. 1983. *Language Games and Activities*. Amersham, England: Hulton.

Hadfield, C. and Hadfield, J. 1990. *Writing Games*. Walton-on-Thames, England: Nelson.

Miller, L. and Rogerson-Revell, P. 1993. 'Self-access systems'. *ELT Journal* 47(3):228–33.

Rinvolucri, M. 1984. *Grammar Games*. Cambridge: Cambridge University Press.

Sheerin, S. 1989. *Self Access*. Oxford: Oxford University Press.

CHAPTER 12

Self-Access Language Learning for Secondary School Students

Julie Forrester, The British Council, Hong Kong

INTRODUCTION

The summer of 1993 was the first time that the British Council in Hong Kong ran the Intensive English Language Programme for students entering Form 7. This course was designed to help these students bridge the gap between Chinese-medium secondary schools and English-medium tertiary education. There were approximately 1,100 students with a teacher-student ratio of 1 to 10. The course was run at two centres (the Institute of Language in Education and City Polytechnic of Hong Kong), both of which had a centre supervisor, and a self-access supervisor.

The first part of this paper summarizes reports from the *South China Morning Post*, in order to show the 'political' background to the course. The rest of this paper is a description of the course, as it developed from the planning stages through to classroom practice.

BACKGROUND

According to the Hong Kong Examinations Authority (undated), only about 18% of students sitting for the Hong Kong Certificate of Education Examination in English, Syllabus A (which is made easier for Chinese middle school candidates) obtain a grade C or above.

There has always been debate about why this should be so: it may be that Chinese school students' lack of proficiency in English has its roots in the curriculum and that this cannot be remedied by short courses. Nevertheless, the Education Department gave HK$10 million for the first year of operation of a four week intensive summer course to boost the English of students from Chinese-medium schools.

The British Council was appointed to manage the course, which very broadly followed the syllabus of the A-Level Use of English exam, supplemented with oral and listening practice. The course was taught by both expatriate and local teachers.

The Deputy Director of Education, Robert Lo Chun-hang has said on various occasions that some Chinese-medium school students were rejected by universities only because of their poor English. A bridging programme therefore was necessary to raise the competitiveness of students from Chinese-medium schools and thus eliminate parents' fears that Chinese middle school graduates were educationally inferior.

The students who took the course will sit for the Use of English examination to qualify for admission to universities. Students who still cannot meet this English standard despite finishing the course will be offered an extra six-week training session during the following summer holiday and another exam. A pass in the supplementary test will be treated as the equivalent to a pass in A-Level English, qualifying the student to be admitted to tertiary institutes.

THE COURSE

The course was 120 hours long, five days a week for four weeks, and was made up of four main components: approximately one-sixth self-access; two-sixths integrated skills activities; one-quarter reading and writing/text study; and one-quarter oral, listening and grammar activities. Almost all the materials were specially written for this course by teachers at the British Council with the exception of the writing activities textbook 'Writing 3' (Littlejohn 1993).

The course was not intended to have the kind of grammar or vocabulary input which schools already offer: instead it was designed to focus mainly on the macro skills needed for tertiary level study, such as an understanding of text and paragraph structure and organization.

A second focus of the course aimed to develop the students' responsibility for their own learning. To this end, self-access was timetabled into the course for one hour per day, totalling twenty hours which were to be spent mostly on listening and reading. The part of the course which was self-access consisted of extensive reading and listening, and at the beginning of the course there was a self-awareness component to help students analyse their needs and show them how and where they could meet those needs locally. They were also given a list of local resources and asked to grade them in terms of personal convenience, interest and usefulness. During the self-access slots, there was always a self-access supervisor or assistant on hand as well as the class teacher.

LISTENING

The self-access listening, like the classroom listening, aimed to provide a variety of accents on the same general topic: themes for self-access listening included 'My Home Town', 'Unusual Hobbies' and descriptions of how organizations are managed, with extended narratives and prompted monologues all specially recorded for the self-access tapes. It was found that radio programmes were not appropriate for use as they were often too predictable, from the point of view of question writers, or required too high a level of vocabulary and linguistic competence. Most of the material was only very loosely scripted, if at all, so that the English was as 'real' as possible, true, personal, and including hesitation and unfinished sentences.

For self-access listening, each student received their own copy of a 'SALLY' (Self Access Listening Library for You) tape containing around forty minutes of specially recorded materials. These were divided into three sets of worksheets, each to be completed over a period of one week, so that it would be possible for students to complete some of the work at home. From a purely administrative point of view, it was also hoped that encouraging a student to use his or her own cassette player would take some of the pressure off the number of available tape recorders during the timetabled self-access slots.

At the end of each week the students received an answer key and a tapescript (for scripted material) and to encourage frequent listenings, there were also generic worksheets, with questions such as 'Who is speaking?' or ' What do they discuss?' which focused on overall gist.

READING

For the self-access reading, there were 100 specially written worksheets with answer keys. Almost all of the texts were taken from English language Hong Kong newspapers, for which permission to copy had been obtained. The aim was to encourage extensive reading (hopefully, for pleasure) as well as intensive reading, and the questions covered the sub-skills of prediction, skimming and scanning, with some guessing of meaning combined with dictionary work. Although there were teachers available while the students were working on these passages, the questions and answer keys had to be written in simpler language than the texts themselves if the students were to cope with them on a genuinely self-access basis.

During the materials writing process, several modifications were made in the style of the reading worksheets. If the answer key to a question refers to a specific paragraph, students should be able to pinpoint the reference easily, so the paragraphs of all the articles were numbered. The reading worksheets had a 'To Think About' section at either the beginning or end. If this section was at the beginning of the worksheet it acted as a prediction or pre-reading task. When this section was included at the end of the worksheet it took on the form of a discussion or personal opinion type questions. Both these activities worked well, although placing 'To Think About' at the beginning of the article seemed to be preferred as it activated the students' schemata and got them into the article easily.

SPEAKING

The students were encouraged to practice 'extended talking' with their teachers during their self-access periods. There was always a teacher in the room to supervise the activities and speaking to them took on several forms:
–   the students had to ask questions about getting started on certain of the activities;
–   the teacher was involved in refereeing language games or other disputes in the group;
–   some students just came up and started chatting to the teacher.

ORGANIZATION AND SUPERVISION OF MATERIALS

Before the self-access materials were written, certain decisions had to be made about the format that would be used, as this would later influence any system of filing. All the self-access reading worksheets were made by pasting the original newspaper article onto an A4 sheet, with the questions usually typed on the same page. For longer articles, the headline or photo was often put onto a separate sheet, but it was felt that if the body of the article would not fit onto an A4 sheet, then it was too long and would not be used. By choosing articles which were at the maximum A4 in length we had some control over the amount of time the students would spend on reading an article — if the articles were too long this might demotivate the students.

The worksheets were labelled with a general category, such as 'Hong Kong', 'Relationships', 'Health', and then given a unique identification number within that category (thus 'Health 01', 'Health 02', etc.) for filing. The originals were then laminated and distributed to both centres.

Although it was left to centre self-access supervisors to decide on the storage system, it was suggested that all the articles in one category could be stored together, perhaps in plastic envelopes, and the whole selection stored in plastic boxes or trays. The plan was for students to look at the laminated copies to select a category and a particular worksheet that they were interested in, and they would then be given a photocopied version of the article and the questions, without the answer key. Once they had showed the tutor or self-access supervisor on duty that they had answered the questions, they would then be given the pre-prepared answer key for comparison and checking. The answer keys were designed to be self-explanatory, but there would always be two or three tutors at hand to answer any queries. Self-access supervisors were expected to do stock-keeping so that there was a record of the most popular worksheets as well as an adequate supply of photocopies.

To encourage students to look at the whole range of categories, they were asked to consider whether they agreed with this categorization or if they could think of more appropriate labels. This involved students in making decisions about the materials and providing useful feedback to the tutors on which materials were being used. Multiple readings of the same text were also promoted by a generic worksheet with questions like 'Is this article an event report, is it a feature article (giving an opinion) or is it a description?' This type of skimming or gist question also served to focus on the overall structure of the text and its organization.

CONCLUSION

This paper has described some of the characteristics of introducing self-access study to a group of secondary school students on an intensive language course. Several points should be highlighted:
- look for material that is easy to adapt into self-access;
- try to encourage students in some aspect of material selection or preparation;
- ensure that there is always a teacher on hand to solve problems or encourage the students;
- be organized but be flexible.

It is hoped that our experiences at the British Council can be of use to other individuals or organizations as they incorporate self-access language learning into an existing syllabus or future course.

ACKNOWLEDGEMENTS

Erica Laine was in charge of the project. Jonathan Chamberlain wrote most of the course. Olha Madylus and John Hall wrote the listening component. Julie Forrester wrote the self-access reading component.

REFERENCES

Hong Kong Department of Education (undated). *Comparability Study Between TOEFL and CE English Language.*

Littlejohn, A. 1993. *Writing 3: Cambridge Skills for Fluency.* Cambridge: Cambridge University Press.

CHAPTER *13*

Incorporating Aspects of Style and Tone in Self-Access CALL Courseware

Lynne Flowerdew, Language Centre, Hong Kong University of Science and Technology

INTRODUCTION

This paper reports on a computer-assisted language learning (CALL), self-access, job-seeking skills package designed for both undergraduate and postgraduate students at the Hong Kong University of Science and Technology (HKUST). The CALL exercises are based on an error analysis of students' letter and résumé writing and address three main areas of weakness: style and tone, grammar and lexis. However, it is the area of style and tone that is the main thrust of this paper as this type of error was found to outnumber those concerning grammar and lexis, and was deemed to be the most serious because of the potential offence it might cause the recipient. Moreover, this area was also chosen as hitherto, this has been a largely neglected area in CALL courseware design where the focus tends to be on syntax and grammatical accuracy at the expense of fluency and appropriacy. As a follow-up to the error analysis, both undergraduate and postgraduate students were informally interviewed to try to determine the source of the errors pertaining to appropriacy. In addition, a local Hong Kong instructor[1] and American/Canadian instructors in the Language Centre at HKUST were consulted on ambiguous points of style and tone at the materials writing stage.

The first part of this paper details the error analysis stage with particular reference to style and tone. The second part outlines the various components of this self-access package and gives a brief overview of the authoring programs which are matched with the different writing tasks in the job-seeking procedure. Each exercise typology in the authoring program is then described to show how it has been manipulated to incorporate features of style and tone. The paper concludes with suggestions for dealing with some cross-cultural issues which became evident during consultations with students in the error analysis stage, and with language teachers in the materials design stage.

ERROR ANALYSIS

An error analysis of the letter-writing module of a business communications skills course for forty undergraduate students was carried out over one 15-week semester. Five different types of business letters (letter of enquiry, acceptance, rejection, appreciation, confirmation), concerning correspondence between a supplier and client company regarding a proposal as part of a simulation activity, were analysed for common errors relating to appropriateness and style. Informal follow-up interviews were also conducted in order to determine the cause of such errors.

Students were extremely fond of using clichés and jargon, e.g. *Thank you for your co-operation and attention.* Another such stereotyped phrase that frequently occurred was: *With reference to the above-captioned.* . . . When questioned about these, students said that they intuitively felt that these expressions were over-used, but resorted to them as they could not think of anything better to substitute them with. Another reason given was that they were taught such expressions in secondary school. Interestingly, those students with work experience maintained that clarity and conciseness were not always viewed as aspects of a good writing style within the Hong Kong business environment. They pointed out that as far as the middle-aged, Hong Kong Chinese business people are concerned a stereotyped phrase such as *Please find herewith enclosed* . . . is considered more appropriate than the expression *I enclose.* . . .

Many errors also centred on the two aspects of appropriacy: formality and directness, with students failing to distinguish between formal and less formal phrases, e.g. *Please don't hesitate to* . . . and *Please feel free to* . . . . In this respect, lexical choice was also problematic as students could not differentiate between the different degrees of formality of near-synonyms, e.g. *opportunity* and *chance*, *job* and *post*, and *discuss* and *talk about.*

In general, students tended to overuse the more tentative expressions equating them with politeness while disregarding their appropriateness in a particular context. For example, students would use *I would be very grateful if you could send me* . . . for a simple request when an expression such as *Would you please send me* . . . would suffice. Another typical comment was 'What's wrong with: *You are kindly requested to* . . . instead of, *Could you please* . . . everyone recognizes this phrase and besides it sounds more polite.' Moreover, those students with work experience also mentioned that if they omit such clichés and over-polite expressions from their letters, their bosses have instructed them to insert these to make the letter sound more 'businesslike'. One student mentioned that she had been instructed by her boss to commence 'thank you' letters with the formulaic expression *I am writing to express my heartfelt gratitude . . .* On the other hand, students also went to the other extreme by being too direct when a more circuitous expression was called for. For example, very few students were able to write a tactful letter of rejection as they were unfamiliar with the conventional practice of softening the 'bad news' by embedding it in positive information.

There were also several instances of long-windedness, with students failing to use reduced relative clauses because they reported they were unfamiliar with this stylistic convention.

The main problem with the résumés was that they sounded rather 'flat' as the students didn't really try to sell themselves but presented the information in rather a matter-of-fact way (e.g. *I was a member of the Drama Society*) rather than persuasively (e.g. *Took a leading role in two plays*). Students commented that they used such expressions as *I was a member of . . .* and *I was responsible for* because they were familiar with these and unaware that action verbs, such as *Took* could be used to improve the tone of the résumé, thereby 'selling' themselves by highlighting their achievements.

Such comments from the students obviously pose problems for the design of materials. The author's initial reaction was to deprogramme the students from using such jargon and over-polite phrases as these contravene the usual conventions associated with good writing. However, if the omission of such stereotyped phrases renders the letter 'unbusinesslike' in the eyes of the local Hong Kong manager, then the letter may well not achieve its purpose and, in this case, result in an unsuccessful job application. The job-seeking skills package, while promoting a clear, concise and appropriate native-speaker type writing style, also has to take account of this local linguistic phenomenon. Therefore, caveats could be included in the CALL exercises alerting students to the fact that some employers may insist on a more old-fashioned style of writing.

COMPONENTS OF THE JOB-SEEKING SKILLS PACKAGE

The following writing tasks have been identified as the most salient written elements of this package:
1. Making the initial enquiry: writing off for an application form and further details.

2. Writing a short cover letter to accompany the application form and résumé.
3. Writing an application letter: solicited and unsolicited.
4. Constructing a résumé.
5. Replying to a job offer: accepting and declining.

The above list was arrived at after an analysis of job advertisements in the two local English language newspapers, reference to business text-books specifically written for the local market (Bentley 1991) and consultation with students at HKUST seeking help from the Writing Centre with job application letters. As regards writing application letters, the focus is on unsolicited letters, or rather 'semi-solicited' ones, as a large percentage of students appear to write letters as a follow-up to general recruitment drives conducted at HKUST rather than in response to specific jobs advertised in the press. A letter declining a job offer is also included in this package because, as a lot of 'job-hopping' takes place in Hong Kong, there is a reasonable chance that a job-seeker may well apply to the same company on another occasion and by writing a courteous letter declining an offer will have left a favourable impression.

DESCRIPTION OF AUTHORING PROGRAMS

The job-seeking skills package was implemented using *Testmaster, Gapmaster, Storyboard, Choicemaster* and *Matchmaster*, all from the Wida suite of authoring programs (Jones and Trackman 1988, 1992). Testmaster is the most versatile in the suite as it allows teachers to model several exercise types and can give the most comprehensive feedback. The exercise types to which it easily lends itself are: question and answer, sentence completion, expansion from keywords, jumbled words, and sentence transformation (e.g. active to passive). Gapmaster is used to write cloze exercises, whereas Storyboard while following the same principle blanks the entire text thus removing any contextual help. Choicemaster is used to construct multiple-choice exercises and is interactive as it allows feedback messages for student responses. Matchmaster presents different kinds of pairs to be matched by the student user.

Appendix 1, a cover sheet for student reference which gives a breakdown of all the material, illustrates how each particular program has been matched with a specific writing task. It should also be pointed out that this package has been targeted at three different types of end-users. It is expected that the majority of students wishing to make use of this package will be final-year science and business students with no full-time work experience. Another group consists of post-graduate students of whom about a quarter have previously been in full-time employment. A third potential group of users are those undergraduates from any year who are applying for part-time vacation work or a job placement. The brief notes on each application letter listed on the cover sheet in Appendix 1 reveal how an attempt has been made to cater for each category of student.

IMPLEMENTATION OF AUTHORING PROGRAMS

This section describes, with reference to each writing task, how each authoring program has been exploited to address students' weaknesses in style and tone as revealed by the error analysis.

Initial Enquiry (Testmaster)

For the initial letter of enquiry, students have to reconstruct a phrase from prompts:

I/apply/post/Assistant Marketing Manager . . .

All possible options e.g. *I am writing/I wish/I would like to apply* . . . have been built into the answer key as potential responses. The program also allows a maximum of three error messages with a number of options within each. For example, if students wrote *I'd like* . . . or *I'm writing* . . . an error message would alert them not to use short forms in formal business letters. Likewise, if students wrote *I want* . . . or *I desire* . . . they would be given feedback on the inappropriate use of the verb. Students are also advised against using dull and over-used openings such as *With reference to (the above-captioned post)*. Lau (personal communication)[1] has pointed out that it is not sufficient to merely advise students against using such clichéd phrases; they also have to be convinced as many local textbooks advocate use of them. In view of this, some feedback messages have been changed to incorporate this observation and now say that even though some local textbooks present the use of such clichés as good models, they are, in fact, rather old-fashioned and do not adhere to the principles of a clear, concise writing style.

Students have to perform a similar task for the second sentence of the letter:

you/send me/an application form/this post

A hint prompts students to use one modal verb before *you* and to use *please*, taking care with its position in the sentence. The program accepts the modals *could, would, will* and *can,* but if students write *will* or *can,* they are reminded that other modals can be used which sound more polite. A feedback message attached to all the answers mentions that the expression *I would be grateful if you could* . . . should not be used for this simple request. Furthermore, if students place *please* in a marked position at the beginning of the sentence a feedback message instructs them to put it in a more appropriate place.

Short Cover Letter (Testmaster)

The following jumbled word exercise is made more challenging for students as not only do they have to put the words in the correct order, but also delete those which they consider unnecessary.

> completed/requested/forms/with/I/you/the/together/herewith /as/application/testimonials/enclose/have/which

The answer should read: *I enclose the completed application forms together with testimonials, as requested.* If students use *which you have requested* or *as you have requested,* a feedback message prompts them to use a more concise expression. Moreover, if they put the clause at the beginning of the sentence then another message informs them that it is more common to place *as requested* after the main clause.

The last sentence of this cover letter is designed to focus students' attention on the different degrees of formality of lexical items and the force of various modal verbs. Again, this consciousness-raising of appropriacy is achieved by deletion of unnecessary or inappropriate items as in the following example:

> given/interview/possibility/I/will/can/opportunity/the/an/to/I/granted/be/attend/may/hope/chance/would

With regard to lexical items, the program accepts both *opportunity* and *chance,* but informs the student that *opportunity* is a better choice as *chance* is rather informal. *Granted* is marked as an error as it is regarded as too formal an item to use in this context. A hint prompts students to take care with modal verbs. In this instance, there appears to be some conflict between what British and American language teachers regard as appropriate. Whereas British English prefers a tentative modal in the phrase *I hope I may be given the opportunity to attend an interview,* American English favours a more forceful modal such as *will* or *would.*

Both of these differing views of appropriacy have been built into the program, with a feedback message indicating that in British English the tone is considered too strong if *will* or *would* are used, but this is acceptable in American English.

Solicited Application Letter (Storyboard)

When students first see the solicited application letter it is entirely blanked out except for a few given difficult words, and thus provides no contextual help. They can, however, get a substantial amount of help from the job advertisement itself to enable them to decode the letter. One area where students fall down is when the job advertisement asks them to state their 'expected salary'. It is common to find students responding to this point with a phrase such as *I expect a salary of* . . . instead of a more tentative expression, e.g. *my expected salary would be.* . . . As mentioned in the error analysis, students' letters are riddled with clichés and jargon and these seem to be especially prevalent in the closing sentence. In order to wean students off using such expressions as *Thank you for your kind attention* or *Thank you for your cooperation,* these gap-filling exercises expose students to a wider variety of closings which are somewhat less clichéd: *I would be grateful if you would consider my application,* or *I look forward to discussing my qualifications with you in person.*

Unsolicited Application Letter (Gapmaster)

In this cloze type exercise, it is important to consider which parts of the text should be blanked out. For example, the error analysis reveals difficulty with lexical choice of near-synonyms. Therefore key lexical items such as *position, post* and *experience* which have a relatively high frequency of occurrence in this letter-writing topic and whose meanings are fairly transparent from the context, have been deleted. The problem students have in this case is not decoding the meaning, but rather making the correct lexical choice to fit a particular collocation. For example, although *job, post* and *position* are practically synonymous, *job* is an inappropriate choice as it does not collocate with *apply* in the following context: *I wish to apply for the Assistant Marketing Manager job.* Items have also been blanked out to draw students' attention to the tentativeness of a suggestion (indicated in brackets), e.g. *I will contact your office in the next few days to discuss the (possibility) of an interview,* instead of the overweening expression *I will contact your office in the next few days to arrange an interview,* which students are apt to use, and which might well cause offence as the applicant is seen to be usurping the employer's position, albeit unwittingly.

Résumés (Matchmaster)

Input on tone in résumé writing is provided through a matching exercise. The introduction explains how applicants should use action verbs (e.g. *established, prepared, supervised)* instead of well-worn phrases (*I was responsible for*) to promote themselves by highlighting their talents and achievements, thus making the résumé more persuasive in tone. In this exercise students have to match eight different statements in one column, with their corresponding action verbs in another column, e.g. *I was responsible for setting up a new system for staff training* would be matched with *Developed.*

Accepting a Job Offer (Testmaster)

The jumbled word exercise in which students are required to delete any unnecessary words has also been used to raise students' awareness of lexical appropriacy. The following example is designed to give students a useful phrase for clarifying/checking information:

starting/month/will/understand/be/I/salary/that/ $8,000/know/pay/ per/my

The answer should read: *I understand (that) my (starting) salary will be $8,000 per month.* The brackets indicate the elements are optional. If students use *know* or *pay* they are informed that there are more appropriate items they can use.

Declining a Job Offer (Choicemaster)

'Bad news' messages (e.g. declining a job offer) typically display a somewhat complex information structure pattern where the unfavourable news is de-emphasized by being embedded in positive information. The error analysis revealed that students were unfamiliar with this writing strategy and expressed the news too directly. Exercises were developed which attempt to remedy this lack of understanding of the cognitive structuring of propositional content in a letter declining a job offer. The following question is taken from such an exercise:

Which sentence below would be the most suitable continuation of 'I am very pleased to be offered the computer analyst position.'

(a) However, I have been offered a position with another company.
    Message: It's a good strategy to offer a reason before declining the offer, but this lead-in is a little too direct.

(b) However, I am writing to say that I will not be able to accept your offer.
    Message: Avoid a direct rejection. The best strategy is to use a tactfully-worded reason to prepare the reader for the 'bad news'.

(c) And I deeply appreciate the hour you spent talking with me at the interview.
    Message: This sounds insincere.

(d) However, during my job search I applied to three other highly-rated firms like your own.
    Message: This acts as a good lead-in for the reason. The use of 'highly-rated' will lessen the impact of the rejection. Avoid using 'esteemed' as this is rather old-fashioned.

The local Hong Kong Chinese do not give a specific reason for rejecting a job offer[1] and instead will use the following tactical phrase: '*Due to (For) personal reasons. . . .*' This observation has been included in the feedback message.

Additional Exercise on Style and Tone (Choicemaster)

As the two complementary aspects of appropriacy, i.e. strong vs. tentative and formal vs. informal, are such a problematic area for students a supplementary exercise was devised to cover the most common problems exposed by the error analysis. Two example questions appear below:

Which is the most appropriate phrase for giving your contact number?

(a) Please feel free to contact me on . . .
    Message: Incorrect tone — 'feel free' has a similar meaning to 'please don't hesitate to', but is more informal. These phrases have the function of giving permission and are more likely to be used by a superior to a subordinate.

(b) Contact me on . . .
  Message: Add one word to sound more polite.

(c) Please don't hesitate to contact me on . . .
  Message: Tone is appropriate, i.e. you sound polite. But this phrase has the function of giving permission and is more likely to be used by the employer to the applicant.

(d) I can be contacted on . . .
  Message: This states the information neutrally, without overtones of 'giving permission'. 'My contact number is . . .' and 'Please contact me on . . .' are also acceptable alternatives.

The last paragraph of a job application letter should ask for action (i.e. an interview). Which is the most appropriate expression below:

(a) I look forward to the opportunity of an interview.
  Message: This is a polite, concise expression.

(b) I would be extremely grateful if you would kindly consider my application.
  Message: This sound too begging and over-sincere. Use adverbs such as 'extremely', 'kindly', 'highly', 'greatly' with care.

(c) It would be highly appreciated if you would consider my application.
  Message: Avoid this awkward phrase. Use 'I would appreciate it if or 'I would be grateful if . . .' instead.

(d) I will phone you to find out the date of the interview.
  Message: This is too direct and therefore sounds aggressive.

CONCLUSION

This paper has attempted to demonstrate how the aspect of style and tone has been incorporated in CALL courseware for self-access use. One innovative feature of this program is that the exercises are highly needs-oriented as they are based on an error analysis of students' writing. One of the interesting findings to surface from the consultations with students in the error analysis stage, and a local Hong Kong language teacher and American/Canadian teachers in the materials writing stage, was the ten-sion between what the author and the other stakeholders considered as appropriate style and tone. The British author tended to favour the more tentative expressions whereas the American teachers went for the more aggressive, self-promoting ones. The author's original intention was to promote a clear, concise writing style free of clichés and jargon whereas the students showed a predilection for these over-used expressions citing the preference of the local, middle-aged Hong Kong managers for such old-fashioned, verbose language. One cannot ignore these culturally-based linguistic phenomena in such a culturally-diverse city as Hong Kong; accordingly, these different linguistic realizations have been accommodated within the CALL exercises and perhaps the best advice one can give to students is to remind them to always bear in mind the audience they are addressing and to adjust and fine-tune their message accordingly. It is also hcped that this paper will, through its discussion of exercise types and provision of examples, give CALL practitioners some ideas for exploiting authoring software to incorporate this neglected dimension of style and tone.

NOTE

1. I wish to thank my colleague, Pansy Lau Lam Mi-ying, for her invaluable feedback on the exercises in this CALL package. Her insights and suggestions for refinement have enhanced the overall quality of the courseware.

REFERENCES

Bentley, M. 1991. *Mary Munter's Business Communication — Strategy and Skill. (Open Learning Institute of Hong Kong)*. Singapore: Simon and Schuster.

Jones, C. and Trackman, I. 1988. *Choicemaster, Matchmaster*. Computer Authoring Programs. London: Wida Software Ltd.

————. 1992. *Gapmaster 2, Storyboard 2, Testmaster 2*. Computer Authoring Programs. London: Wida Software Ltd.

APPENDIX

Material in Job-Seeking Skills Package

This package consists of the following letters and practice material which are available in the programs listed on the right. The exercises can be done in any order. Choose the ones which are the most relevant for your situation.

* Initial enquiry + layout   Testmaster
    (i.e. writing in for application form)

* Cover letter   Testmaster
    (sent with application form)

* Style and tone in application letters   Choicemaster

* Application letters   Storyboard
    (solicited, i.e. in response to an advertisement)

    Letter 1: suitable for an M.B.A. student
    Letter 2: suitable for a science undergraduate or new graduate with some vacation work experience
    Letter 3: suitable for a science graduate

* Application letters   Gapmaster
    (unsolicited, i.e. sent on your own initiative)

    Letter 1: suitable for a science student graduating soon
    Letter 2: suitable for an undergraduate business and management student. Written in response to a recruitment drive.
    Letter 3: suitable for a science post-graduate student with some full-time work experience
    Letter 4: suitable for an M.B.A. student with some work experience
    Letter 5: suitable for an undergraduate student. Written in response to a recruitment drive.

* Résumés   Matchmaster
    (using action verbs) (language structures)   Choicemaster

* Declining job offer   Choicemaster

* Accepting job offer   Testmaster

From English Teacher to Producer: How to Develop a Multimedia Computer Simulation for Teaching ESL

Linda Mak, English Language Teaching Unit, The Chinese University of Hong Kong

INTRODUCTION

This paper describes the stages involved in developing a piece of multimedia courseware and suggests a framework for teachers who may be interested in this new technology for language teaching purposes. The paper first explains the rationale for designing a multimedia computer simulation (1997 Dilemma) for tertiary students in Hong Kong. It then briefly outlines the stages the author, an ELT teacher, has gone through in developing such a program. It also discusses the problems identified in the pilot stage and offers suggestions for the development of multimedia courseware.

BACKGROUND

During the establishment of a new Independent Learning Centre (ILC) at the Chinese University of Hong Kong (CUHK) it became clear that many ESL learners and teachers are not satisfied with the text-based type of computer-assisted language learning (CALL) software which is most commonly available; users need meaningful language practice software. It also became clear that although multimedia technology has enabled the computer to integrate audio, video, visual and text components together in a package, very limited authentic and communicative software has taken advantage of this facility. A survey conducted at CUHK reveals that undergraduate students are highly interested in authentic topics and current affairs (Lai and Mak 1992). Students also want more listening and vocabulary practice. This has motivated the author to develop a multimedia computer simulation game based on a controversial topic of current concern.

Hong Kong will become part of China in July 1997. This has been and will remain a major issue. Current tertiary students here have to confront the issue and to decide whether to stay in Hong Kong, or to emigrate. Many students are, however, distancing themselves from the issue for various reasons, for example: fear of uncertainty, lack of self-confidence and a sense of inertia. In order to challenge students to think about their future and to encourage them to communicate their feelings and views with one another, a new channel has to be sought. Computer simulation was chosen because it is motivational and real (Carrier 1991). It is hoped that a multimedia computer simulation will serve as a starting point for communication both through oral discussion in ELT classes, and through written communication via an on-line forum for both students and staff in the ILC.

PROJECT PREPARATION

Course Objectives and Program Design

The four design principles of interactive video described by Jones (1991) are equally applicable to computer simulations:

1. Devise a scenario that creates opportunities to practise the target behaviour.
2. Try to reconcile the narrative sequence with the desired learning sequence.
3. Let the criteria for success or failure in the simulation be determined by the learning objectives.
4. Integrate instructional procedures, such as presentation of text, comprehension checking, feedback and help, into the scenario. (Jones 1991: 242–3)

Scenarios for 1997 were created, based on the envisaged problems that might be encountered by people staying in Hongkong and those who are emigrating. Throughout the program, users are invited to decide whether they will stay or leave. This not only forces users to think, but also allows interactivity because each response branches to a different storyline. This emphasizes that users decide their own fate. There is no concept of success or failure in the simulation. Each individual decision is personal and should be respected. The chief aim is to alert the users to the possible consequences of their decisions.

It was important to decide which elements of language learning to incorporate in the project. Students value listening practice so the simulation had to involve a lot of aural work such as news reports, debates, forums and dialogues. Reading was limited to two screenfuls to avoid straining the eyes of students and also boring them. It was decided to include short newspaper clippings and headlines on-screen and leave long texts in a file of supplementary readings.

Vocabulary was the secondary language focus. It was decided not to include vocabulary aid or translations but on-screen keywords were included.

Carrier's (1991) four-phase approach for each cycle of the simulation[1] was modified slightly as follows:

1. on-screen instructions;
2. decision-making and consequence-bearing;
3. journal writing (for reflection and sharing);
4. off-screen in-class discussion and on-line self-access communication through electronic mail forum;
5. summary/report writing.

To avoid the problems of hangman-type exercises (decontextualization of vocabulary and limited potential as a conversation catalyst) and the lonely learner syndrome in CALL and self-access learning, an electronic mail forum was added as a follow up. It creates a new environment for discussion (anonymously and on a self-access basis) and increases fluency in writing as well as encouraging written communication among student and staff users both inside and outside the ILC.

Independent follow-up to 1997 Dilemma takes the form of narrative (users report on what they chose, encountered and felt, instead of simply 'what we did'), essays (posted to the on-line forum) and summary reports of the electronic mail interaction.

Script Writing

Initially there was no major funding for this project. It relied on ILC funded student helpers. A student helper did a library search and wrote up the script. The first draft took about two months. The following three months were spent on collecting feedback from colleagues and students and constantly revising the script.[2]

Co-ordination

The computer centre of CUHK co-operated in this project, with their assistance the following tools were chosen:

Development Tools

Hardware: Quadra, video card (Video Spigot)
Software: Macromind Director (program), Photoshop (scanning and visual effect), Adobe Illustrator (charts, table and text), Sound Edit (digitize and edit sound), Adobe Premiere (video).

Delivery Platform

LCIII or above, with at least 16 Mb memory, 8 bit colour display, 50 Mb disk space, quick time extension, System 7 or above, a pair of external speakers and a 13 or 14 inch monitor; optional compact disk drive and earphones.

PRODUCTION

Production was regulated by a schedule, a production table and a location-shooting table. For convenience and financial reasons, the pilot version was taped by volunteer students and staff in various settings: at home, in their offices, etc. It took over two weeks to finish all the audio-segments.

Two student helpers were recruited to collect visuals and trained to assist in scanning, sound digitizing and program script writing, however, most of the graphics and presentation work still relied heavily on the media technician. Searching for graphics to support the idea, editing and synchronization of audio and visual parts are the most time-consuming tasks. The computer work itself took a minimum of two weeks.

PILOTING

The pilot version was tried out using two ELT classes of thirty-two students in total. It was used in a lab in the computer centre with small groups of three to four students. The program was run on three different models of Macs (LCII, IIvx and Quadra 700) to test how the speed and the quality might affect the presentation. Pre- and post-viewing questionnaires were completed by each student, followed by a face-to-face discussion in one class to collect immediate feedback. The students actively participated in the debriefing of the simulation, criticized intelligently the problems of the script and gave constructive suggestions on how to revise it. They also exchanged individual views on the 1997 issue.

A number of teaching staff, from both the English Language Teaching Unit of CUHK and other departments, were invited to try out the simulation and to discuss how the program could be improved. This provided a lot of insights. Piloting with students and staff feedback contributed to the identification of four main problem areas.

Scripting

This was the source of the main problem. The script had been revised over six times before it was taped. However, many students and staff viewers reflected that some simulated problems were not relevant or challenging enough. Also, as the topic was so 'recent' things kept changing every day, the data selected for the simulation became quickly out-dated.

Sound Quality

The audio segments were taped in various venues without the supervision of someone with production experience or expertise. The sound quality was inconsistent and a few dialogues were marred by undesirable noise and distractions. This led to problems with one of the course objectives, i.e. listening comprehension in an everyday life situation with background noise.

Technical Constraints

A lot of audio and visual components were involved, this took up a lot of disk space: 38 Mb for 8-bit pictures on IIvx and 70 Mb for 16-bit pictures on the Quadra. The LCII could not support Quicktime videos and the pictures were downgraded to 8-bit, resulting in poorer quality. Also, the files were large and not compressed which resulted in long loading times, sometimes the screen was blank for over 10 seconds.

Funding

Funding for the audio-taping in the studio and the scriptwriting had to be sought from the university. The program did not have high commercial value despite the professional presentation and although the content focuses on individual choices rather than the political aspect, the whole issue is so politically sensitive that it would be time consuming and troublesome to persuade the university to allow the product to go to press. Moreover, the issue is so imminent that it may lose its market value after 1997. Furthermore, macintosh computers are not common in Hong Kong. These factors demotivate the commercial publishers and affect the funding of the project.

REVISION

To improve the script, a few scenarios were rewritten or updated, making them more relevant to the learners. The wording of the questions was revised so that they became clearer and more compelling. To strengthen the language learning side, more choices and on-line help were added. Help buttons were added to enable learners to choose to listen only, to listen with the key expressions on screen, to read the script or to look up the meaning of the key expressions in the glossary. All the audio segments were retaped in a studio. This has satisfactorily improved the quality. With the experience now accumulated, the taping took less than three hours (for a 30-minute final output).

The computer centre attempted several solutions to the technical problems. Finally, by repositioning the questions, they reduced screen transition time to two or three seconds and added graphics to fill the blanks between files. Everything was compressed and the required disk space was reduced to 28Mb. Only 20% of the pilot version could be reused. As some scenarios were changed and everything retaped, the audio part had to be redigitized. In addition, the audio, the visuals and the text had to be re-synchronized. Funding was still a problem so full-time staff completed this revision stage.

FUTURE DEVELOPMENTS

A second part of the package, 'Hong Kong Pathfinders' has been initiated by a colleague and preparation for its production is now under way. This is an ambitious three-level package which includes a lot of interesting game devices such as jigsaw reading, social identity test, scoring, slaying of 'ideological' monsters,[3] on-line writing, etc. With some difficulty, a professional scriptwriter and a voluntary professional producer have been found to bring the simulation to a more thought-provoking level. Funding remained a problem at first. Fortunately, after integrating the software into a research project, the project was finally funded by CUHK.

Unlike many organizations which link CALL with language classes, the ILC is restricted to self-access learning. The usage rate is definitely lower. Moreover, though bimonthly talks have been arranged to promote the use of Internet, electronic mail, concordancing, etc., a number of language teaching staff are still very sceptical or even resistant to CALL. Thus it is important to not only develop multi-media CALL software, but also to justify its value and effectiveness to the learners, the teachers and the university.

A BROADER PERSPECTIVE FOR THE PROJECT

Where and How to Start

Experience shows that the pedagogical design is the most important and the most difficult part, followed by artwork (synchronization and library search). The computer work is comparatively easy. Practitioners should start by defining their objectives, things to be considered are:
- The kinds of language skills to be enhanced.
- The kinds of task that learners are required to complete in their study and future careers.
- The kind of guidance, feedback or interaction the computer provides.
- The link between the program and the curriculum or the other self-access or CALL materials available to users.
- The requirement for additional learning materials, e.g. program guide and text-files.

The level of a teacher's computer knowledge is of little importance, of more importance is to decide: in what ways computers are really better than other media in achieving goals; what the limitations are; and whether use of the medium is cost effective. It is important to understand the needs of the learners and the institution, they may not always match.

Practical questions such as the place of delivery and funding should not be overlooked. It is useless to spend precious time on producing a program but then find there is nowhere the student users can work on it. Institutional support is essential too. Support from colleagues, the department and the computer professionals must be real. This involves teamwork in the production stage and the pilot stage, as well as the willingness to integrate the product into the curriculum.

Expenses

The major investment is staff hours. The project described here has taken a year to complete. The student helper spent over 200 hours on script writing and revision[4] and the computer staff invested several weeks. Time for promoting the software to students and for moderating the on-line forum has yet to be counted.

Staffing

Fleischman (1990) suggests that a basic multi-media software development team should consist of at least a writer, a software author and a media technician, each with special responsibilities and expertise. The writer's responsibility is to establish the goals and objectives of the course, design the pedagogical model and to collect information from classroom instructors. It is also his job to collect and synthesize this information to fit the software design. The software author's role is to establish the navigation path — the user interface that determines how the learner moves through the course. The role of the media technician is to use various media building blocks to create the necessary graphics, images and sounds.

The project described here also started with a team of three. A student helper acted as a scriptwriter. A language teacher capitalized on classroom experience and the survey of students' needs to set the course goals/objectives, design the simulation, and coordinate the audio-taping and program development. A media technician brought to the project experience with video production and also had the support of computer officers.

This division of labour was not as first envisaged. The author expected to design the simulation and edit the script only, leaving the computer centre to deal with audio and video taping as well as the computer work. It became more complicated than that. The author became involved partly in the writing and software development. In addition, it was necessary to co-ordinate a number of exchange students and colleagues to do the audio-taping.

Moreover, the pilot and guest viewing all pointed to the need for a more experienced professional scriptwriter to handle such a controversial and sensitive topic. It was also clear that a professional producer was needed to take charge of the audio-taping in the studio and to participate in the visual presentation.

CONCLUSION

There are benefits to be gained from multimedia courseware production. Firstly, the range of instructional materials will be enriched through using modern technology. Secondly, invaluable experience will be gained about producing multimedia CALLware and the related constraints. Hopefully, colleagues will be motivated to work together to produce other new courseware. Finally, much is to be gained by networking with, and learning from the expertise of computer professionals, language experts, professional scriptwriters, etc. This will prepare the ground for future production.

Multi-media computer courseware production is an art, it provides new ways of presenting but is extremely time-consuming and requires a team of experts from various fields. Even with the support of a computer/media technician, the teacher may need to take up the roles of scriptwriter, program designer, co-ordinator, or even producer. The year spent on this project is not to be regretted because the project is innovative and the issue is worth supporting. However, other teachers should think twice before embarking on such a project. This path should only be followed if would-be developers have a very communicative topic and cannot find anything to satisfy their needs on the market. Above all, developers should not wait until every detail is worked out, or every problem is solved, otherwise their dreams will never come true. The important things to remember are: start with the objectives, get focused on the language side, build a production team, get the ball rolling towards the common goal and finally, get started.

NOTES

1. Carrier's four phases are: preparation for decision-making, keyboard practice, reactive decision and follow-up development task.
2. The revision period was long because both the author and the scriptwriter were heavily involved in other teaching/studying duties. With a professional scriptwriter, the process may take about two weeks.
3. These monsters include: power without morality, politics without principles, knowledge without integrity, etc.
4. This may be much reduced if the writer is a teacher or a professional writer. The first level of Part II only took the professional scriptwriter two weeks.

REFERENCES

Carrier, M. 1991. 'Simulations in ELT: a cooperative approach'. *Simulation and Gaming Journal* 22:224–33.

Fleischman, J. 1990. 'Macintosh multimedia building blocks'. *CÆLL Journal* 1(1):7–9.

Jones, G. 1991. 'Some principles of simulation design in interactive video for language instruction'. *Simulation and Gaming Journal* 22:239–47.

Lai, E. and Mak, L. 1992. 'A preliminary report on students' attitudes towards the ILC'. *Occasional Papers in ELT*:1–18. The Chinese University of Hong Kong.

Section Four

Evaluating Self-Access

CHAPTER 15

Learning to Improve: Evaluating Self-Access Centres

Marian Star, Institute for Language in Education, Hong Kong

INTRODUCTION

Current initiatives in the teaching and learning of English as a Second Language in Hong Kong have recognized the need to take account of developments in educational theory and practice which stress individual differences and learner independence. These developments have been practically realized in the establishment of self-access centres for language learning. The huge investment in establishing and maintaining these centres makes regular evaluation essential.

This paper outlines the principles which underpin self-access learning and relates them to the purposes and methods of obtaining feedback in self-access centres. A case study of an evaluation carried out in the self-access centre of the Institute for Language in Education is then described.

Researchers such as Knowles (1975), Hermann (1980), Gardener (1985) and Skehan (1989) have stressed the importance of individual differences in learning and provided an impetus for the movement towards individualization. In turn, this has influenced the development of practices aimed at providing individual learners with choices. Early efforts to individualize were characterized by a choice of content only. However, later efforts offered learners a range of choices which included pace and method of learning as well as a choice of content. More recently there has been a surge of interest in finding a methodology that provides choice while at the same time encouraging learners to accept responsibility and develop independence. In response self-access learning has developed. It has been defined by Riley et al. (1989) as a 'system' of learning where different learners, working on different activities, enjoy different degrees of self-direction within a particular and unique institutional context. Centres which have been specially designed to provide a physical backdrop for this method of learning have increased in Hong Kong over the past few years. However, as those who are already involved with self-access centres well know, the huge financial outlay for establishing centres does not necessarily ensure that the aims of this mode of learning are met. It is now time to assess just how successful these centres are in meeting the needs for which they were established.

PURPOSES AND METHODS OF EVALUATION

Self-access systems are difficult to evaluate for two reasons. Firstly, they are highly complex. For example, learners, helpers, materials, the organization and administration, design and layout all combine to form a system for learning based on principles of individualization and learner independence. It is a dynamic and vital system requiring the interdependence of each and every aspect. Secondly, every self-access system is unique because of the institutional context in which it is established. The type and needs of learners as well as the objectives, finances and physical setting of the institution combine to form a unique context. For evaluation this means there are any number of areas on which to obtain feedback. It is, therefore, essential at the outset to clearly determine the purpose for which feedback is sought and, once this has been identified, the method used to obtain the feedback will follow.

In general, the broad purpose of evaluating is to develop and improve all aspects associated with the quality of learning and teaching (Nunan 1988; Thorpe 1988). However, because of the complexity and uniqueness of self-access systems it is desirable to make more explicit the purposes for which feedback is sought.

Riley et al. (1989) distinguish two specific purposes for obtaining feedback in self-access systems; for the purposes of management and for the purpose of measuring the success or failure of the system.

The former requires 'a collection of facts' often presented in the form of a report and used as justification for financial support for future development. Number of users and patterns of use, for example, might be justification for an increase in manpower or for more equipment.

On the other hand, feedback for the purpose of assessing the success or failure requires a broader 'evaluation' of the system. This type of feedback can be obtained directly through questionnaires and interviews or indirectly from observations. The data are then related to the objectives for which the self-access centre was established. It is, therefore, essential that objectives for the centre are clearly defined. These may give priority to such areas as language improvement, where success or failure on test scores can be used as feedback for the purpose of evaluation. Alternatively, priority may be given to developing independent learners, in which case questionnaires and observation techniques might form the basis of feedback for the evaluation.

With specific reference to self-access, Sheerin (1991) makes even more explicit the purposes for which evaluations are conducted. She distinguishes two purposes, both linked to specific objectives. The first is to measure the effectiveness of self-access as a learning environment and the second is to determine the effect self-access has on students.

One way to evaluate self-access as a learning environment is in terms of the success of students learning the foreign language (Dickinson 1987), while another is to look for 'signs of change' in learners such as level of awareness, change in attitudes towards learning and styles of learning (Sheerin 1991). However, as Sheerin (1991) explains, these methods are only suitable in situations where the centre's objective is to learn a foreign language and where it is possible to distinguish self-access as the only mode of learning.

This paper, however, concentrates on evaluation for the purpose of assessing what effect self-access has on students by asking learners themselves to rate the facilities of the centre. This is appropriate in cases where the objective of the centre is to develop learners' self-direction and independence. Evaluation of this type can be conducted on a broad scale by looking at users' access to the various facilities offered in the centre or, on a smaller scale, by investigating a single aspect, such as the role of consultations.

CASE STUDY RATIONALE

The centre evaluated is part of the Institute of Language in Education which offers in-service refresher courses for teachers of English as a Second Language. The self-access centre was established in 1991 with the dual aims of providing facilities for language improvement and encouraging self-direction and independence. As in-service teachers could only spend a limited amount of time on the course (sixteen weeks), it became increasingly obvious that the priority for the self-access centre should be the development of learners' self-direction and independence so that they would be able to continue their own post-course language improvement. It was also thought that by emphasizing the principles of self-direction and independence learners might transfer these to their classrooms when they returned to teaching.

Although the centre seemed to be functioning reasonably well after two years of operation, informal feedback from users indicated that more could be done by way of helping them to better use the facilities of the centre. It was felt that if students were hindered in their access to the centre they would also be hindered in exercising self-direction and independence. It was useful, therefore, to identify what it was that actually helped or hindered access so that existing facilities could be improved.

Four main areas of access were investigated. The first looked at the kind and type of learners using the centre. The second asked students to rate their level of access in relation to their level of satisfaction with the orientation programme given as an introduction to the centre. The third area looked at the usefulness of various features of the centre such as colour coding, instruction and answer sheets, etc., and the fourth looked at what improvements students themselves recommended in order to help their access.

METHOD OF EVALUATION

Quantitive data were collected using two questionnaires. The first was divided into three parts dealing with:
1. Learner kind and type, this included previous experience of self-access centres and independence in learning, experience of English (e.g. competence, use and contact with native speakers) and learning behaviours.
2. Level of satisfaction with the orientation programme, (e.g. information booklet, learning contract, briefing sessions, orientations to equipment, layout and help to choose learning units) and the usefulness of various features of the centre (e.g. colour coding and instruction, and answer and progress record sheets).
3. Learners' priorities for recommended improvements (e.g. helpers on duty in the centre, guidelines for identifying needs and level, materials for checking progress and strategies for learning).

Parts 1 and 2 asked students to rate their responses on a scale of 1–5.

Questionnaire 1 was completed shortly after students started using the centre. Questionnaire 2, which reused Parts B and C of Questionnaire 1, was completed towards the end of the Refresher Course after approximately sixty hours of self-access. While information from the questionnaires would indicate what hindered or helped students in their access it would not provide sufficient insight into the reasons why this was so. Group interviews were, therefore, organized to gather qualitative data to help explain the results.

SUMMARY OF RESULTS

Learner Type

Despite the fact that the small sample size (69) made it difficult to draw firm conclusions, there are indications that certain kinds and types of learners have better access to the centre. Although no relationship was found between students who reported previous experience of self-access and experience of independence the interviews showed that they cannot be ruled out as possible contributing factors to facilitating access. Students (7) who said they had used a self-access centre before had little idea of what constituted a self-access centre equating it with a room set aside for completing homework and assignments. Only one student had previously used an actual centre for a period of three months. Similarly, for experience of independence it was found that at least 60% of students reported previous experience of decision-making in courses but this, on the whole, amounted to only single decisions for single courses and was associated with limited choices presented to them rather then real choices generated by them.

When experience of English was correlated with level of satisfaction with the orientation programme it was found that students who had more contact with native speakers and those who reported a higher level of English competence had better access to the centre. Students reporting more contact with native speakers were more satisfied with the course descriptions in the information booklet when they began the course. Contact with native speakers, therefore, may provide an increased level of exposure to English which enables better comprehension of information in the booklet and so provides better access. Students who rated themselves as having a better level of English competence were found to be more satisfied with time spent on their own looking through materials in the centre. These students are likely to be more confident and, therefore, content to browse independently. It is interesting, however, to note that this relationship was only found for Questionnaire 2 which was completed at the end of the course. The fact that it was not indicated in Questionnaire 1 may be attributed to the newness of the experience of self-access for the vast majority of students who, despite their level of competence, were unsure of what was expected of them when the course began. Once students had become more familiar with their new mode of learning and more confident in their new environment, where English was spoken all the time, the relationship between experience and time on one's own emerged.

Learning behaviours that were shown to have influenced better access were those of initiating conversations with teachers or others and using grammar books. Students who are prepared to initiate a conversation are less dissatisfied with orientation sessions to the self-access centre because they are more likely to articulate any queries they might have and, therefore, stand a better chance of understanding the whole operation of the centre.

Students who used grammar books reported that they found the tutor's introductory briefing session more satisfactory than students who did not. This session relies heavily on the course information booklet and the tutor provides more details where necessary. It is likely that students who are used to looking for information in grammar books find less difficulty matching the two sources of information. Students who use grammar books also reported that instruction sheets and model answers were useful, possibly because they were used to looking for information and also because much of their previous learning experience in Hong Kong would have utilized grammar exercises with answer keys.

Also, students who said they liked to work alone found the descriptions of the course units in the information booklet more satisfactory. This may be because these students are more independent learners and therefore find the information booklet useful when working on their own to plan their programme.

Orientation Programme and Features of the Centre

There was a general endorsement of the orientation programme and features of the centre. At the beginning of the course students were moderately satisfied with all aspects of the orientation programme and agreed that almost all features of the centre were useful. The mean scores for Questionnaire 2 also show a general endorsement, despite the fact that students are clearly dissatisfied with the language laboratory orientation and level of help to choose units of work (Table 1). When Questionnaires 1 and 2 were compared it was found that access was helped most by the description of units in the information booklet and colour coding to indicate language level, and was hindered most by the lack of information received in the language laboratory orientation and the use of guided answers for feedback (Table 2).

Improvements

An overwhelming majority of students, both at the beginning and end of the course, rated guidelines for language level and language needs as the two most necessary improvements to the centre. These were followed by information about learning strategies, materials for assessing progress,

**Table 1 Comparison of Satisfaction with Orientation Programme
(results of paired t test)**

	Q1 %Satis.	Q1 Mean[1]	Q2 %Satis.	Q2 Mean	t VALUE
Description of units	47.8	3.54	40.6	3.36	2.25* p < .05
Brief by tutor	53.6	3.51	31.9	3.16	3.69* p < .001
Language Laboratory	27.5	3.07	14.5	2.78	2.86* p < .01
Self-access Centre	44.9	3.48	33.3	3.33	1.60
Time on own	36.2	3.20	28.9	3.00	1.94* p < .06
Help	42.0	3.36	18.8	2.93	4.26* p < .001
Learner Agreement	41.8	3.37	26.5	3.00	3.84* p < .001

[1] For Mean, the higher the score, the more 'satisfied'.
* is significant at p < .05 level.

Table 2 Comparison of Evaluation of Features of the Centre (results of paired t-test)

	Q 1 % Agree	Q1 Mean	Q2 % Agree	Q2 Mean	t Value
Different colours	85.5	1.74	89.9	1.68	0.44
Program sheets	69.6	2.13	60.9	2.39	-2.60* p < .05
Instruction sheets	72.5	1.99	60.9	2.33	-3.45* p < .005
Model answers	82.6	1.78	81.2	1.81	-0.23
Guided answers	17.4	3.23	18.8	3.29	-0.40

[1] For Mean, the higher the score the more the 'disagreement'.
* is significant at p < .05 level.

colour coding for language-skill areas and information about new materials in the centre (Table 3). This gave a clear indication of what aspects would lead to improved access for them.

In the interviews, 13 students said they had received some help to identify language needs while 19 said they had received no help. All 32 students interviewed said they had received no help to identify language level and felt some guidance would have saved them time and effort in searching for suitable materials. Also, all students interviewed said they

Table 3   Comparison of Priorities for Improvements to the Centre

	Q 1 % Necessary	Q 1 Mean[1]	Q 2 % Necessary	Q 2 Mean
Colour coding	(4) 73.9	2.16	(4) 73.9	2.09
Tutor on duty	(8) 55.9	2.37	(6) 65.2	2.28
Strategies on instruction sheets	(3) 82.6	1.77	(3) 76.8	2.07
Map	(9) 46.4	2.52	(8) 58.0	2.45
Guides for language needs	(2) 89.9	1.71	(2) 87.0	1.83
Guides for language level	(1) 92.8	1.70	(1) 89.9	1.78
Materials to assess progress	(4) 73.9	2.12	(4) 73.9	2.06
Newspaper section	(7) 56.5	2.38	(7) 63.2	2.28
Speaking section	(6) 60.9	2.19	(6) 65.2	2.20
Information about new materials	(5) 66.7	2.09	(5) 72.5	2.07

[1] For Mean, the higher the score, the higher 'unnecessary'.
 ( ) = priority

would like training in cognitive as well as metacognitive strategies. On both questionnaires, top priority was given to guidelines for needs and level, with strategy training receiving second priority. This is a strong indication that training in these areas is particularly lacking and should be a top priority for any future developments in the centre.

Approximately 75% of all students on both questionnaires indicated their need for materials to help check progress. If success in language learning is linked to motivation, either as a cause or as a result (Burstall 1975; Gardener 1980), then knowing how much progress has been made is an important element in independent learning and an essential element of self-access learning.

WHAT HAS BEEN LEARNED

While it was heartening to find that students had a moderate level of access to the centre, it was more than clear that the centre was deficient in providing adequate training for the kind of learners using the centre. These learners generally had no previous experience of self-access or independence, had a low level of experience of English and used a variety of learning behaviours and styles. They were, therefore, learners who needed help to find out how they could learn best using the facilities provided.

Further evidence that the lack of training created serious problems for access was found when the two questionnaires were compared to see if using the centre over a prolonged period of time increased access (Tables 1 and 2). It was expected that students would become more familiar with the facilities of the centre over time and would, therefore, have better access towards the end of the course. However, the mean scores for satisfaction with the orientation programme and usefulness of the features of the centre actually decreased over time, indicating that in fact access declined.

The reasons for this may be twofold. The first is that the majority of students, who were unsure of their language needs and learning styles at the beginning of the course (in the interviews only 10 of the 32 students could articulate their needs), became more aware of these as their use of the centre increased. With their language requirements more clearly formulated students, when asked to reflect on the orientation programme and features of the centre, considered that more could have been done to help them learn, even though they had felt moderately satisfied with these areas when they embarked on this mode of learning.

The second reason why access declined may be due to students' increased awareness of their role as learners. The increased realization that responsibility for learning rests with them is matched with the realization that this is only possible when support, which allows them access to facilities for independent learning, is provided.

Students' recommendations for improvements to the centre also strongly point to the need for learner training. The fact that these users give top priority to the necessity for guidelines to identify language level and language needs leaves little doubt that training is essential for access.

CONCLUSION

If learner independence is the aim of teaching and learning programmes, the physical setting where this activity takes place must, as far as possible, allow for individualization and encourage independence. Evaluating self-access centres by asking students to rate their access is a valid method of determining whether the aims of independence have been met as centres are only effective in relation to the level of access they provide for learners to exercise this independence.

Learning what helps or hinders access is useful but must be coupled with the planned implementation of improvements. To this end, the self-access centre at ILE started a vigorous programme to improve learner training. This includes making the information booklet more accessible to the majority of students by improving its design, layout and readability and including more information on the principles and practice of self-access learning; standardizing orientations to the various facilities of the centre, such as the language laboratory and computers, so that all students receive the same input; providing students with an introductory talk on the principles of self-access learning; and improving consultations by explaining their purpose to both students and tutors and asking tutors to be more proactive in this area. There is also an experiment under way to provide more formal learner training by helping learners raise their awareness of reasons for learning and how to learn best. At present this training is given to only one-third of the students for two hours at the beginning of the course with a view to introducing this to all students in the future.

Various features of the centre are also being improved and these include simplifying instruction sheets, explaining the use and value of guided answers and including a range of methods and materials for students to monitor their progress.

Learning about self-access centres in order to develop and improve the quality of the system of learning and teaching that operates within them is an on-going process. There are always different learners with different needs, new tutors, new technologies and new materials, all of which make regular evaluation an essential part of ensuring the vitality and development of self-access learning.

REFERENCES

Burstall, C. 1975. 'Factors affecting foreign language learning: a consideration of some recent research findings'. *Language Teaching Abstracts* 1–21.

Dickinson, L. 1987. *Self-Instruction in Language Learning*. Cambridge: Cambridge University Press.

Gardener, R.C. 1985. *Social Psychology and Second Language Learning*. Britain: Edward Arnold.

Hermann G. 1980. 'Attitudes and success in children's learning of English as a second language: the motivational vs. resultative hypothesis'. *ELT Journal* 34:247–54.

Knowles, M. 1975. *Self-Directed Learning*. New York: Association Press.

Nunan, D. 1988. *Syllabus Design*. Oxford: Oxford University Press.

Riley, P., Gremmo, M. and Moulden, H. 1989. 'Pulling yourself together: the practicalities of setting up and running self-access systems', in D. Little (ed.) *Self-Access Systems for Language Learning*. Dublin: Authentik.

Sheerin, S. 1991. 'Self-access'. *Language Teaching* 24(3):143–57.

Skehan, P. 1989. *Individual Differences in Second Language Learning*. London: Edward Arnold.

Thorpe, M. 1988. *Evaluating Open and Distance Learning*. Essex: Longman.

CHAPTER 16

Directions for Research into Self-Access Language Learning

Lindsay Miller, English Department, City Polytechnic of Hong Kong and
David Gardner, English Centre, The University of Hong Kong

INTRODUCTION

Kershaw (1993) paints a gloomy picture of the future of self-access language learning (SALL). He compares SALL facilities to those of language laboratories in the 1960s and in doing so reminds us of the earlier comments of Stern (1983:64) who declared that the 'introduction of the language laboratory was undertaken with virtually no systematic research except on its engineering aspects. The teaching methodology was developed ad hoc, and what research was done was after the event.' Kershaw goes on to state that the comparison between language laboratories and self-access centres is justified in that both are resource-based rather than theory- or needs-driven. Therefore, unless we ground our work in SALL on serious research rather than over enthusiastic, well intentioned but insubstantial investigations Kershaw's prediction that SALL facilities may be a passing fad could well become true.

The aim of this paper is to direct the reader's attention to areas within SALL where research is urgently needed. The urgency lies in the fact that many self-access centres (SAC) are established at great expense by institutions whose plans are based for the most part on teacher intuition rather than carefully researched data. Research needs to be carried out for several reasons:

1. There is a dearth of solid research reported in the literature.
2. Not all language teachers are convinced of the value of self-access for their students, quality research might alter their perspectives on how languages are learned.
3. Research into effective learner training will contribute to the greater involvement of learners in their learning.
4. Self-access learning is not a major part of the training of language

teachers. This situation will only change when teacher trainers have
been convinced of its importance.
5. Set-up funding is usually available for SALL facilities, however, recur-
    rent funding is more difficult to secure without the ability to demon-
    strate (with substantial data) the usefulness of the facilities.
6. Research funding is frequently conditional on the successful outcomes
    of previous research.

There is a lot of published research within language learning. Researchers
of self-access now have two tasks, firstly to identify the existing research
which has useful implications for SALL and secondly, to identify the areas
that are missing from the literature and which need to be researched to
develop a better understanding of SALL. The rest of this paper addresses
the second task.

PHILOSOPHIES OF SALL

SALL may become unique within language training mainly because of the
many different approaches that can be taken to establishing it. As yet no
one theory exists to say how we should implement SALL and there is still
a great deal of confusion as to whether it is the same as learner autonomy. Much research is still needed into this area. This research must
be conducted with a methodology which is adaptable to specific situations because of socio-cultural difference between groups of learners. The
small amount of literature that is available mostly originates from Western countries. This raises the question of whether these ideas can be
transformed directly into other cultural contexts, e.g. the SACs which are
springing up in a number of south-east Asian countries.

   Enforcing Western beliefs about language learning on different cultures may cause problems which become more obvious in a learner-cen-
tred approach. These beliefs, if not in harmony with the host culture, will
become an obstacle to effective learning. Richards and Lockhart (1994)
set out a series of beliefs which are important to consider when approach-
ing learner autonomy, these beliefs are:
–   Beliefs about the nature of English.
–   Beliefs about speakers of English.
–   Beliefs about the four language skills.
–   Beliefs about teaching.
–   Beliefs about language learning.
–   Beliefs about appropriate classroom behaviour.
–   Beliefs about self.
–   Beliefs about goals.

Richards and Lockhart maintain that the learner's belief system may not match that of the tutor. If this is so, then the SALL facilities which we offer for language learning may have little or no effect. This whole area of learners' beliefs about language learning and how SALL can be accommodated within these beliefs has yet to be researched. This research will then lead onto a more grounded theory, or theories, of SALL without which much of the time and effort invested in setting up self-access centres may be wasted.

LEARNER TRAINING

In many educational systems throughout the world learning is mostly, if not entirely, teacher-centred. To suddenly change the study habits of learners is asking too much of them. We must investigate effective ways of helping learners to develop efficient independent-study habits. This can be achieved in a number of ways: familiarising learners with self-access centres; sensitising them to their learning strategies; engaging the learners in discovery activities about independent learning; encouraging them to make decisions about their language learning; asking the learners to reflect on what they are doing. Such activities are already in use in a number of SACs and have led to a number of small scale studies (see Ma, Martyn, Moynihan Tong, Pang and Or in this volume). Studies based on large scale data collection approached in a systematic way are still missing from the literature.

In addition to the areas mentioned above there is also a need to investigate other aspects of learner training. Of particular importance are:
1. The effectiveness of learner training programmes, for example, whether learners react to intensive learner training, or whether integrating learner training activities into regular class lessons would be more effective.
2. When to begin learner training.
3. The length of learner training programmes.
4. The type of learners who react best to learner training, for example, categorized by age/sex/area of study/motivation.

TEACHER DEVELOPMENT

We must not only attempt to investigate ways of making learner training effective but also consider the human resources we have to work with, namely the tutors in an institution. We need to consider how to train the tutors to be effective learner trainers. Bailey (1994) mentions that when working in a learner centred methodology there are possible problems the teacher may have, these are:

1. Working with a flexible curriculum generates a lot of stress.
2. Teachers need a wide range of skills that were not part of their training.
3. Teachers need support and assistance when working in a learner-centred approach.

Some form of tutor assessment needs to be carried out to find out if the staff in an institution are prepared to be involved, and involve their learners, in SALL. If staff are interested but unskilled in the area of learner training we have to consider how best to meet their needs.

MATERIALS

When considering the materials for SALL we must be aware of the system of self-access in use in an institution. We then have to consider how the system of self-access dictates the materials that are necessary for it to be an effective system. Investigating systems will help us to gain a broader perspective of the type of materials which are necessary for SALL.

Materials development is already a sophisticated area within language learning. Many of the insights gained from research in this area are applicable to self-access materials development. There are also other areas of research which are exclusive to SALL materials development. Some of the areas to be considered are:

1. Whether some types of material produce greater learning in self-access mode than others.
2. The relationship between class-based materials and those placed in SACs.
3. The applicability of commercially produced materials for SALL.
4. The effectiveness of in-house materials production.
5. The special features of SALL materials.
6. The classification of SALL materials.
7. The benefits of student generated materials in SALL.
8. The motivational value of authentic materials.
9. Overcoming the difficulties of using authentic materials.
10. Print-based support for technology-based materials.

TECHNOLOGY

In many cases SACs have attracted technology. This is often because of the ease with which administrators can be persuaded of the need for a technological approach to self-access learning. Technology may be an attractive prospect for administrators who see it as being cheaper than human resources in the long term. As SACs have attracted technology, we must seriously consider the uses to which it can be effectively put in developing SALL. Some of the areas that need to be researched are:

1. The cost effectiveness of in-house production of CALL materials.
2. The cultural appropriateness of existing audio/visual materials.
3. The usefulness of satellite TV and other live broadcasts.
4. The adaptability of technology for SALL.
5. The inhibition factor of technology on non-technology literate learners.
6. The data collection potential of technology in SACs.
7. The potential for increased interactivity between the learner and the learning-materials.
8. The utility of providing learners with self-record facilities (audio and video).
9. The effects of passive versus active video viewing on language development.
10. The attractiveness of technology to the learner.

EVALUATION

When talking about the AMEP National Curriculum Project in Australia, Nunan (1989:23) concludes that ' ... curriculum development requires a collaborative approach between the different stakeholders in the educational process.' A similar situation exits with self-access. There are many stakeholders and each wants to know how the SALL facilities are working. For funding bodies we need to be able to give some form of concrete data. We need to address issues like:

1. Who uses the SALL facilities.
2. How often the facilities are used.
3. How often the materials and resources are used.
4. The outcome, in terms of language learning.
5. Whether SALL effectively supplements other modes of instruction.

Many of these questions would be of interest to the tutors involved in SALL. They would also be interested in obtaining more practical data on how the learners are learning. Issues of interest include:

1. The type of materials most suitable for SALL users.
2. Ways to help motivate or help sustain motivation of the users.
3. The best seating/table arrangements.

4. The most suitable location for different types of materials/facilities.
5. Whether learners take the independent skills they are learning to use in the SAC and use them in their language class or in their independent study outside of the centre.

When considering evaluation it is important not to forget the evaluatory needs of the learners. Their main requirement is always to know: 'How am I doing?' Research needs to be conducted to establish the most effective way or ways of providing this feedback.

One method of providing learner feedback that has been researched is self-assessment. This area has been extensively written about (see Blanche and Merino [1989] for a review of the literature), however, many of the studies reported on contradict each other as to the effectiveness of self-assessment: some studies show it can be done by students while others show students are unable to assess their own language learning ability. We need to investigate the whole area of self-assessment in SALL carefully before we encourage our learners to attempt this. The consequences of allowing learners to perform their own self-assessment when they may have difficulty in doing so would result in the SALL facilities being used inappropriately and may lead to demotivating students and hence the under use of the facilities.

A further important area of research is that of evaluating the effectiveness of SALL materials. Classroom teachers are fortunate in that they receive immediate feedback on the effectiveness of the materials they are using. Without a proper system of evaluation built into their materials production methods, self-access materials writers may never know if their materials are being used effectively or, in some cases, even if they are being used at all.

RESOURCES

Availability of resources, both material and human, undoubtedly affect the way in which self-access is conducted. It is possible that in many cases, lack of large scale resources has prevented teachers from developing self-access in their institutions. However, even with a limited budget, restricted space, unconvinced colleagues and learners who are new to self-access it is still possible to provide a small scale self-access facility which is of use to learners (for example see Tibbetts in this volume). Carefully documented studies are needed into the ways in which SALL can be adapted for less favourable conditions. Reports of these studies will be of interest throughout the language teaching community.

Within public education it is often the case that self-access is developing more rapidly and is better funded in tertiary than in secondary institutions. Finding ways to help secondary institutions develop self-access, even on a small scale, is of equal importance to tertiary teachers as they inherit the student products of the secondary system.

Tauroza and Miller (1992) discuss the possible symbiotic relationship which could exist between tertiary level institutions and company training centres, a similar relationship could also be fostered between tertiary and secondary institutions. This would then have ramifications on the system of SALL facilities and the materials they hold. Research is needed into this possible relationship and its implications for future self-access development.

CONCLUSION

This paper has tried to shed light on many of the areas which still need investigation and research before we can truly say that SALL is a viable alternative or supplement to classroom-based language teaching. It is hoped that the points made will encourage many SALL practitioners around the world to add a research dimension to much of the work they are already doing. Little extra effort is required to document, analyse and evaluate on-going development projects. The results of such research, when published, will be of benefit to all those currently struggling to set-up, maintain and justify the existence of SALL facilities.

In addition to making data collection a routine part of SALL development it is hoped that at least some researchers will be able to conduct large-scale, in-depth projects. Such research projects may, at first sight, be unattractive to many teachers because of the long term commitment which is inevitably involved. However, the positive aspect of such projects is the excitement of working largely in uncharted waters and the consequent increased value of the findings. Many of the issues raised in this paper would make worthy topics for post-graduate dissertations or theses.

Unless we do conduct more thorough research into SALL, both the areas mentioned in this paper and others, we may find that self-access centres are treated the same way as language laboratories were in the 1960s and become nothing more than a passing fad (Kershaw 1993).

REFERENCES

Bailey, K. 1994. *The Teacher's Role in Learner Centred Methodology.* Paper presented at the fourteenth Thai/ TESOL conferences. Bangkok, Thailand.

Blanche, P. and Merino, B.J. 1989. 'Self-assessment of foreign-language skills: Implications for teacher and researchers'. *Language Learning* 39(3):313–40.

Kershaw, G. 1993. 'Self-access centres: the fads and the facts'. *Thai TESOL Bulletin* 5(4):48–58.

Nunan, D. 1989. 'Towards a collaborative approach to curriculum development: a case study'. *TESOL Quarterly* 23(1):9–25.

Richards, J.C. and Lockhart, C. 1994. *Reflective Teaching in Second Language Classrooms*. New York: Cambridge University Press.

Stern, H.H. 1983. *Fundamental Concepts of Language Teaching*. Oxford: Oxford University Press.

Tauroza, S. and Miller, L. 1992. 'In-company trainers, tertiary level ESP teachers and self-access language learning: the case for collaboration', in T. Boswood, R. Hoffman and P. Tung (eds.) *Perspectives on English for Professional Communication*. Hong Kong: City Polytechnic of Hong Kong.

References

Allan, M. 1985. *Teaching English with Video*. Essex: Longman.

Bailey, K. 1994. *The Teacher's Role in Learner Centred Methodology*. Paper presented at the fourteenth Thai/ TESOL conferences. Bangkok: Thailand.

Baker, A. 1977. *Ship or Sheep*. Cambridge: Cambridge University Press.

Bella-Dora, D. and Blanchard, L.J. 1979. *Moving Toward Self-directed Learning: Highlights of Relevant Research and of Promising Practices*. Alexandria, VA: ASCD.

Benson, P. 1992. 'Self-access for self-directed learning'. *Hong Kong Papers in Linguistics and Language Teaching* 15:31–7.

Benson, P. 1993. 'How to be a better language learner: a learner preparation programme for self-access'. Paper given at the ILEC Conference on Language and Learning, The University of Hong Kong, December 1993.

Bentley, M. 1991. *Mary Munter's Business Communication — Strategy and Skill. (Open Learning Institute of Hong Kong)*. Singapore: Simon and Schuster.

Blanche, P. and Merino, B.J. 1989. 'Self-assessment of foreign-language skills: Implications for teacher and researchers'. *Language Learning* 39(3):313–40.

Blue, G.M. 1988. 'Self-assessment: the limits of learner independence', in A. Brookes and P. Grundy (eds.) *Individualization and Autonomy in Language Learning*. ELT Documents 131: The British Council.

Bossert, S. 1988–89. 'Co-operative activities in the classroom', in E.Z. Rothkopf (ed.) *Review of Research in Education, Volume 15*. Itasca, IL: F.E. Peacock Publishers.

Bowler, B. and Cunningham, S. 1991. *Headway: Pronunciation*. Oxford: Oxford University Press.

Bradford, B. 1988. *Intonation in Context*. Cambridge: Cambridge University Press.

Broder, C., Brown, K., Forester, B. and Kaufmann, R. (undated) 'Parispanny Adult and Community Education Centre, workshop materials'. Cited in A. Wenden, 1991. *Learner Strategies for Learner Autonomy*. Prentice Hall International.

Brookfield, S. 1985. 'Self-directed learning: A critical review of research', in S. Brookfield (ed.), *Self-directed Learning: From Theory to Practice* (New Directions for Continuing Education, No. 25). San Francisco: Jossey-Bass.

Brown, G. 1977. *Listening to Spoken English*. London: Longman.

Brown, G. and Yule, G. 1983. *Teaching the Spoken Language*. Cambridge: Cambridge University Press.

Burstall, C. 1975. 'Factors affecting foreign language learning: A consideration of some recent research findings'. *Language Teaching Abstracts* 1–21.

Carrier, M. 1991. 'Simulations in ELT: A cooperative approach'. *Simulation and Gaming Journal* 22:224–33.

Carvalho, D. 1993. *Self-access: Appropriate Material*. Manchester: British Council.

Cooper, R., Lavery, M. and Rinvolucri, M. 1991. *Video*. Oxford: Oxford University Press.

Dickinson, L. 1987. *Self-instruction in Language Learning*. Cambridge: Cambridge University Press.

Dickinson, L. 1992. *Learner autonomy 2: Learner Training for Language Learning*. Dublin: Authentik.

Dickinson, L. and Carver, D. 1980. 'Learning how to learn: steps towards self-direction in foreign language learning in schools'. *ELT Journal* 35(1):1–7.

Ellis, G. and Sinclair, B., 1989. *Learning to Learn English*. Cambridge: Cambridge University Press.

English Pronunciation Dictionary. 1992. Cambridge: Cambridge University Press.

Falvell, J. 1979. 'Metacognition and cognitive monitoring: a new area of cognitive developmental inquiry'. *American Psychologist* 34:906–11.

Fleischman, J. 1990. 'Macintosh multimedia building blocks'. *CÆLL Journal* 1(1):7–9.

Gardener, R.C. 1985. *Social Psychology and Second Language Learning*. Britain: Edward Arnold.

Gardner, D. 1993a. 'Copyright, publishers and self-access centres' *Hong Kong Papers in Linguistics and Language Teaching* 16:111–5.

Gardner, D. 1993b. 'Interactive video in self-access learning: development issues' in *Interactive Multimedia '93*, Proceedings of the Fifteenth Annual Conference. Washington: Society for Applied Learning Technology.

Geddes, M. and Sturtridge, G. 1982. *Video in the Language Classroom*. London: Heinemann Educational Books.

Gilbert, J.B. 1984. *Clear Speech*. New York. Cambridge University Press.

Greenall, S. 1983. *Language Games and Activities*. Amersham, England: Hulton.

Grellet, F. 1981. *Developing Reading Skills*. Cambridge: Cambridge University Press.

Hadfield, C. and Hadfield, J. 1990. *Writing Games*. Walton-on-Thames, England: Nelson.

Halliday, M.A.K. 1978. *Language as Social Semiotic: The Social Interpretation of Language and Meaning*. London: Edward Arnold.

Harding-Esch, E. 1982. 'The Open Access Sound and Video Library of the University of Cambridge: progress report and development'. *System* 10(1):13–28.

Hart, I. 1993. 'Interactive video in self-access learning: evaluation issues', in *Interactive Multimedia '93*, Proceedings of the Fifteenth Annual Conference. Washington: Society for Applied Learning Technology.

Hermann G. 1980. 'Attitudes and success in children's learning of English as a Second Language: The motivational vs. resultative hypothesis'. *ELT Journal* 34:247–54.

Hill, J.B. 1976. *The Educational Sciences*. Bloomfield, Michigan: Oakland Community College.

Hodge, R. and Kress G.R. 1988. *Social Semiotics*. Cambridge: Polity Press.

Holec, H. 1981. *Autonomy and Foreign Language Learning*. London: Pergamon.

Holec, H. 1987. 'The learner as manager: managing learning or managing to learn', in A. Wenden and J. Rubin (eds.) *Learner Strategies in Language Learning*. London: Prentice Hall.

Hong Kong Department of Education (undated). *Comparability Study Between TOEFL and CE English Language*.

Hymes, D. 1977. *Foundations in Sociolinguistics: An Ethnographic Approach*. London: Tavistock Publications.

Jones, G. 1991. 'Some principles of simulation design in interactive video for language instruction'. *Simulation and Gaming Journal* 22:239–47.

Jones, C., and Trackman, I. 1988. *Choicemaster, Matchmaster*. Computer Authoring Programs. London: Wida Software Ltd.

———. 1992. *Gapmaster 2, Storyboard 2, Testmaster 2*. Computer Authoring Programs. London: Wida Software Ltd.

Kemmis, S. 1985. 'Action research and the politics of reflection', in D. Bond, R. Keogh and D. Walke (eds.) *Reflection: Turning Experience into Learning*. London: Kogan Page.

Kenworthy, J. 1987. *Teaching English Pronunciation*. London: Longman.

Kershaw, G. 1993. 'Self-access centres: The fads and the facts'. *Thai TESOL Bulletin* 5(4):48–58.

Knowles, M. 1975. *Self-directed Learning: A Guide for Learners and Teachers*. New York: Cambridge, The Adult Education Company.

Kress, G.R. and Hodge, R. 1979. *Language as Ideology*. London: Routlege and Kegan Paul.

Lai, E. and Mak, L. 1992. 'A preliminary report on students' attitudes towards the ILC'. *Occasional Papers in ELT*:1–18. The Chinese University of Hong Kong.

Lambert, B. and. Hart, I. 1991. 'Interactive videodisc for the rest of us', in *Interactive Instruction Delivery*, Proceedings of the Ninth Annual Conference. Orlando: Society for Applied Learning Technology.

Laver, J. 1980. *The Phonetic Description of Voice Quality*. Cambridge: Cambridge University Press.

Little, D., ed. 1989. *Self-access Systems for Language Learning*. Dublin: Authentik/CILT.

Littlejohn, A. 1985. 'Learner choice in language study'. *ELT Journal* 39(4):253–61.

Littlejohn, A. 1993. *Writing 3: Cambridge Skills for Fluency*. Cambridge: Cambridge University Press.

Lonergan, J. 1984. *Video in Language Teaching*, Cambridge: Cambridge University Press.

Longman Pronunciation Dictionary. 1992. London: Longman.

Martin, J. 1984. 'Language, register and genre', in *Language Studies: Children writing leader*. 1987. Geelong: Deakin University Press.

Martyn, E. and Voller, P. 1993. 'Teachers' attitudes to self-access learning'. *Hongkong Papers in Linguistics and Language Teaching* 16:103–10.

Martyn, E. and Chan, N.Y. 1992. 'Self-access action research: a progress report'. *Hongkong Papers in Linguistics and Language Teaching* 15:59–68.

McCall, J. 1992. *Self-access: Setting up a Centre*. Manchester: British Council.

Miller, L. 1992. *Self-Access Centres in S.E. Asia*. Hong Kong: Research Report No. 11. Department of English, City Polytechnic of Hong Kong.

Miller, L. and Rogerson-Revell, P. 1993. 'Self-access systems'. *ELT Journal* 47(3):228–33.

Mitchener, D. 1991. 'Setting up a self-access unit'. *MET* 17:(3) and (4):70–1.

Moore, C. 1992. *Self-access: Appropriate Technology*. Manchester: British Council.

Mortimer, C. 1985. *Elements of Pronunciation*. Cambridge: Cambridge University Press.

Nakhoul, E. (1993) 'Letting go', in J. Edge and K. Richards (eds.) *Teachers Develop Teachers Research: Papers on Classroom Research and Teacher Development*. Oxford: Heinemann.

Nunan, D. 1988. *Syllabus Design*. Oxford: Oxford University Press.

Nunan, D. 1989. 'Towards a collaborative approach to curriculum development: A case study'. *TESOL Quarterly* 23(1):9–25.

O'Connor, J. D. and Fletcher, C. 1989. *Sounds English*. Harlow: Longman.

O'Malley, J.M. and Chamot, A.U. 1990. *Learning Strategies in Second Language Acquisition*. Cambridge: Cambridge University Press.

Oppenheim, A.N. 1992. *Questionnaire Design, Interviewing and Attitude Measurement*. Pinter Publishers.

Oxford, R. 1990. *Language Learning Strategies: What Every Teacher Should Know*. Boston: Heinle and Heinle.

Pennington, M. and Richards, J. 1986. 'Pronunciation revisited'. *TESOL Quarterly* 20(2):207–26.

Pennycook, A. 1993. 'Some thoughts on self-access'. *Self-access UPDATE for Teachers* 3:3. English Centre, The University of Hong Kong.

Phillipson, R. 1992. *Linguistic Imperialism*. Oxford University Press.

Pronunciation Plus. 1990. Salt Lake City: MacEnglish.

Richards, J.C. and Lockhart, C. 1994. *Reflective Teaching in Second Language Classrooms*. New York: Cambridge University Press.

Riley, P. 1982. 'Learners' lib: experimental autonomous learning scheme', in M. Geddes and G. Sturtridge (eds.) *Individualisation*. London: Modern English Publications.

———. 1985. 'Mud and stars: personal constructs, sensitization and learning', in P. Riley (ed.) *Discourse and Learning*. London: Longman.

———. 1986. 'Who's who in self-access'. *TESOL France News* 6(2):23–34.

———. 1987. 'From self-access to self-direction', in J.A. Coleman and R. Towell (eds) *The Advanced Language Learner*. London: CILT.

———. 1988. 'The ethnography of autonomy', in A. Brookes and P. Grundy (eds) *Individualization and Autonomy in Language Learning*. ELT Documents 131: The British Council.

Riley, P., Gremmo, M. and Moulden, H. 1989. 'Pulling yourself together: the practicalities of setting up and running self-access systems', in D. Little (ed.) *Self-access Systems for Language Learning*. Dublin: Authentik.

Riley, P. and Zoppis, C. 1985. 'The sound and video library', in P. Riley (ed.) *Discourse and Learning*. Harlow, Essex: Longman.

Rinvolucri, M. 1984. *Grammar Games*. Cambridge: Cambridge University Press.

Rogerson, P. and Gilbert, J.B. 1990. *Speaking Clearly*. Cambridge: Cambridge University Press.

Sheerin, S. 1989. *Self-access*. Oxford: Oxford University Press.

———. 1991. 'Self-access'. *Language Teaching* 24(3):143–57.

Skehan, P. 1989. *Individual Differences in Second Language Learning*. London: Edward Arnold.

Stern, H.H. 1983. *Fundamental Concepts of Language Teaching*. Oxford: Oxford University Press

Sturtridge, G. 1992. *Self-access: Preparation and Training*. Manchester: British Council.

Swales, J.M. 1990. *Genre Analysis: English in Academic and Research Settings*. Cambridge: Cambridge University Press.

Tauroza, S. and Miller, L. 1992. 'In-company trainers, tertiary level ESP teachers and self-access language learning: The case for collaboration', in T. Boswood, R. Hoffman and P. Tung (eds.) *Perspectives on English for Professional Communication*. Hong Kong: City Polytechnic of Hong Kong.

Thorpe, M. 1988. *Evaluating Open and Distance Learning*. Essex: Longman.

Tompkins, C. and McGraw, M.J. 1988. 'The negotiated learning contract', in D. Boud (ed.) *Developing Student Autonomy in Learning*. London: Kogan-Page.

Willing, K. 1989. *Teaching How to Learn*. Macquarie University, Sydney, Australia: National Centre for English Language Teaching and Research.